T0276993

a beginner's
guide
to the universe

a beginner's
guide
to the universe

uncommon ideas
for living an
unusually happy life

mike dooley

HAY HOUSE, INC.

Carlsbad, California • New York City
London • Sydney • New Delhi

Published in the United States by: Hay House, Inc.: www.hayhouse.com®
Published in Australia by: Hay House Australia Pty. Ltd.: www.hayhouse.com.au
Published in the United Kingdom by: Hay House UK, Ltd.: www.hayhouse.co.uk
Published in India by: Hay House Publishers India: www.hayhouse.co.in

Cover design: Kathleen Lynch • *Interior design:* Bryn Starr Best
Images used under license from Shutterstock.com
Photograph on page 167: courtesy of the author

Library of Congress Cataloging-in-Publication Data for the Original Edition

Names: Dooley, Mike, 1961- author.
Title: A beginner's guide to the universe : uncommon ideas for living an
  unusually happy life / Mike Dooley.
Description: 1st Edition. | Carlsbad : Hay House, Inc., 2019.
Identifiers: LCCN 2018049677 | ISBN 9781401955021 (hardcover : alk. paper)
Subjects: LCSH: Life--Miscellanea. | Wisdom--Miscellanea.
Classification: LCC BF1999 .D6152 2019 | DDC 158--dc23 LC record available at
https://lccn.loc.gov/2018049677

Tradepaper ISBN: 978-1-4019-5504-5
E-book ISBN: 978-1-4019-5503-8
Audiobook ISBN: 978-1-4019-5591-5

11 10 9 8 7 6 5 4 3 2
1st edition, March 2019
2nd edition, July 2020

Printed in the United States of America

To Rebecca Solecito Dooley

Before this odyssey ever began,

there was you, your best friends,

and wide-eyed curiosity among you about who would be

the first to leap,

the first to forget, the first to kiss, the first to tell,

the first to fall, the first to get back up,

and the first to remember

that living in the illusions of time and space

all began with a dare . . .

. . . to LOVE in spite of it all.

A portion of the proceeds from the sale of this book will be donated to charity: water.

contents

the man
you
think i am

Dearest Rebecca,

The phone call I'll never forget came late afternoon at home. It was the weekend, I was sitting at the desk in my office, your mother across from me. A nurse began, "You want to know the sex?"

"*What?*"

"You and your wife are having a baby," she explained patiently, "and you want to know the sex?"

"*Yes!* Right!"

Without a hint of emotion, she continued, "You're going to have a girl."

It was as if God had just spoken.

This reality check of our firstborn about to arrive, when I would be 53 years of age, seemed more authentic than the modestly increased curvature of your mother's belly.

A GIRL!

My entire life, while outwardly nonchalant about having kids at all, I'd sometimes allow myself to imagine having a daughter. Of course, by my age, it seemed this boat had already sailed.

And then you arrived, six weeks early. Evading the 25 percent chance you had, based on your mom's and my genetics, of having full-blown cystic fibrosis. Your five and a half pounds turning our family of two into three. Your mother's existence, and mine, about to be transformed in ways unimaginable, never mind that we'd been warned of this by every parent who's ever lived. Even today, my greatest surprise over your presence in our lives is how surprised I've been *by everything*.

As I held you the first time, your searching eyes belied a depth not apparent in your extremely small, frail body. This window to your soul gave no hint of where you've been, the plans you've made, or who you might become. Your tiny limbs and quivering voice were angelic. I was mesmerized. Which had less to do with odds beaten and digits counted, and more with your very embodiment of life's greatest mystery: How could *any* of this—LIFE, YOU, our new family—be *remotely* possible?!

As these first years have rolled by and your fifth birthday now approaches, more than anything else, I'm awed as I witness you taking your place in the world: vessel of spirit, spark of the Divine. Not as "my" child—you are not truly "mine"—but as a child of the Universe. Still confounded that your mother and I somehow caused a biological chain of events, far beyond our ability to grasp, that would deliver you, as if from heaven, into our lives. That we are charged as

 caregivers and light bearers seems so contrarily absurd. Who are we to deserve so much? And who are we to be given so great a task? I fumble in my own darkness enough—there's not much light to spare. Yet, that this madness is so, parents in the dark bringing forth children of light, in a world of *meticulous* order, means there must be a plan and reason for our relationship. And so I will endeavor, as all parents must, to fulfill my role and not take more from you than I'm able to give.

Since your arrival I've adored you for every reason and for none at all. And, as if things could be even
better, to my wild astonishment, you seem to be just
as crazy about me. To the point of embarrassment as
you shun others who crave your attention as much as
I do, and when you reach for me in spite of their out-
stretched arms and open, vulnerable hearts.

Has there been some cosmic mistake that I, rather
than a misplaced saint, am the one so privileged to
enjoy the extreme proximity of your existence and
these mutual currents of adoration, punctuated
with giggles and tears? If only—my heart sometimes
aches—I could be the man you think I am when you
urgently and repeatedly call out, "Daddy! Daddy!
Daddy!" *hundreds* of times in a single day, wanting to
share with me your every observation, idea, or whim.
Or when you cry over my absence, want to ride upon
my shoulders, or sit beside me for a meal. How could *I*
be so important to such perfection as you?

This importance is what I now strive to earn. To
one day become the man you see in me—the man you
think I am—and to always be a light in your darkness,
hope in your despair, and the best father in the world
to any degree I may.

When your mom was still pregnant I was told by a friend that your impending birth would mark the day my life would begin. And so it seems—so much so, that I sometimes feel my time on earth prior to your arrival was merely preparation for what we're now experiencing and all that lies ahead.

Speaking of which, while I have every expectation of loving and guiding you for decades more, I'm not so naïve to think you'll hear all I say, to assume what I offer will actually be helpful, or, to even be sure I'll live that long. Yet, as an author and speaker, whose "Notes from the Universe" have almost made me famous, and whose ideas have at least improved *my* own life, there are some things I hope to impart before this gig is up . . . or before we find out there really was some cosmic mistake. As if, *a beginner's guide to the universe*—a handbook for rocking these hallowed jungles of time and space as a budding master, with uncommon ideas for living an unusually happy life.

Not that I'm a master, but my work the past two decades has been to help people live deliberately and create consciously among life's infinite possibilities—à la *thoughts become things*, my catchphrase in the film and book *The Secret*. I've been teaching that life is neither a random game of chance, nor a test of obedience. That we live in a world of absolute perfection, made possible by love, upon which we are *inclined* to thrive. I actually tell audiences that life is *not* fair, but rigged in our favor.

To add some girding to these otherwise woo-woo ideas, my style and tone have always been more certified public accountant than doting father. I'm simply not used to exploring love and tenderness, which makes all that I feel for you so bizarre and tantalizing. But in spite of my actuarial tone (which I do think serves the lessons), I hope to reach both your mind *and* your heart.

I realize, of course, most people these days don't read books, and I've found this is triply true if the author is a family member. "Never a prophet in your hometown." In your own *home*? Forget it . . . *"and would you please take out the trash?"* That's fine—I'd rather be your dad than your guru. Still, teaching is what I've been doing and loving for 20 years. And, if the things I write could possibly shorten your own learning curves, lessen future suffering, and increase future joys, I must try.

In the pages that follow, there are six chapters covering the key tenets and concepts that I believe, once known, will give you or any reader the biggest boost possible in life. Each chapter is introduced by a letter recalling my own life's epiphanies or relating memories of times recently shared together, followed by brief lessons on taking massive responsibility and its immense rewards. Finally, the epilogue will let you in on the most surprising discovery I've made from compiling these ideas, perhaps even the most surprising discovery of my life, concerning the shortcoming that weighs on me most lately—not being the man you think I am—a revelation with implications for every single person who's ever lived.

So, to spare you any guilt that might arise from blowing off my 15 earlier books, this single one, as simple and concise as I could make it, capturing what I'd most hope any avid reader would gain from all my books combined, is for you . . . and for anyone else who'd like to be reminded of life's beauty, our power, and how much we're loved.

May all that you
wish for
be the least you
receive.

1

why the **sun** rises

Tears and fears filled a large part of your early life.

You still cry for Mumu, though Mom passed when you were one year old. It was her knees you'd cling to when learning to walk. Her 81-year-old frame you'd yearn to hug. Her tired face you'd eagerly kiss.

Three years ago, you screamed, "Daddy! Help! A-a-a-a-a-a-a-a-a-a-a-a-a-g-h!" from the guest bathroom, where moments later I found you, having reached into the empty tub and tipped yourself in, like a seesaw, landing on your extended palms, head down, feet high, your miniature, inverted frame frozen in terror, unable to move except to call for help.

And you woke us on several nights last year, still half asleep, crying with punctuated persuasion, "I . . . DON'T . . . LIKE . . . MONSTERS!"

Crying, obviously, is a child's tribal call for answers, solutions, or love—that, in each case, must be provided by others. Needs that get more complicated as we age, because while we outgrow many of our dependencies, we still find more to be afraid of.

Fear's been my lifelong companion and nemesis. Mostly worrying about things that never happened, my own inadequacy, or what other people are thinking. Yet I've learned how to cope and even to thrive, loved and in love, by discovering that all fears stem from misunderstandings. And that just a few, new, on-point ideas, applied to painful circumstances or sad perspectives, can completely change everything for the better.

The most powerful lesson I may have ever learned came with the realization that at the core of *all fear* lies confusion over *who we really are, why we're here, and what we can do with our lives*. Which may seem unlikely, until you find out those answers. Ironically, when not tragically, the truths we miss that could steer us clear of confusion are easy to observe and experience in our own day-to-day lives.

Our physical senses alone reveal we live in an infinitely kind and unspeakably wise Universe that we are a part of, not apart from; where you, yourself, through mere thoughts, words, and deeds, become a creator. And of our countless creations, our lives are one.

Getting more cerebral, if Einstein was right and reality is merely a "persistent illusion," then by extension, so must be time, space, and matter. He said as much about these elements in lesser-known writings. Which means there are no real "befores," "afters," "nears," or "fars." Everything is literally "here and now," "One," with no spatial, material, or time separations. Such qualifiers merely offer unique windows of selective perception.

So, in a Universe without separations, where all are truly One, mustn't we each be made of, come from, Divine Intelligence? Without separations there can't be God and non-God. Where would non-God "stuff" come from, anyway? And being of God means you, or your higher self, existed "before" this lifetime and you will "after" it; it means you are real, the illusions are not; you are forever, they are fleeting. It means you came first. Yet that you now find yourself within time and space means you (your higher self) must have chosen to be here and now!

To continue using simple logic, we can conversely realize that amid life's staggering sophistication, it's *not* feasible that we're here to be tested, judged, and sentenced by an angry, jealous God. First, a God who could dream up the *entire* universe, much less photosynthesis, could not possibly be so petty, and second, what purpose would testing achieve? To see if God made a mistake?!

Similarly, it's easy to nix the old notion that life started because of some random accident and is devoid of intelligence. That's the same as believing that life sprang from rocks or vacuums, without explaining the origin of rocks and vacuums, while casting a blind eye to the intelligence within the world's 100 million *different species*, and every cell, in their every body.

All of which builds to the inescapable conclusion that *you are important*; sacred, honored, loved, not beholden to a world of illusions; rather, it is beholden to you. You are a creator, through the act of perception, of every rock and vacuum; they did not create you. *YOU are the very reason the sun comes up every day.* Literally. Not "sort of" the reason, but *the* reason. You are free. Just be yourself. There are no tests. All is well. *You deserve happiness, the indisputable highest emotional value known to humankind.* (Love is not an emotion, but an absolute, as you'll read later.) And while these ideas may raise major questions that neither of us has answers for, given the insights just acquired, do those questions matter anymore?

My evidence? How do I know the truth? As your father, I consider it my highest duty to help you think for yourself and to thrive in the world. And to that end, I'm simply offering for your consideration some of the ideas that I've honored and lived to great success. Ideas based on love and respect for all. Hardly my own, yet so universal and self-evident they can easily be attained by any earnest seeker.

My "process" for uncovering truth, which in hindsight always passes a simple two-prong test:

Begin with an idea that electrifies you, sourced from your own experiences, logic, or intuition, and consider it true if it:

- speaks of life's beauty or our power, and

- applies to everyone, always, equally, *no matter what.*

No one is left behind, no one is excluded, no one is judged.

Could there be better confirmations for truth than our own experiences, logic, and intuition? It might be easy to brush these off as amateurish, until you consider that today's predominant beliefs do *not* pass their muster and have no rational basis other than to further scare and manipulate the masses.

If there were better qualifiers of truth, what would they be? Books? Priests? Scientists? Aren't texts, creeds, and theories merely summaries of other people's findings? Better for you to experience life, go within, *draw your own conclusions* and then see how they stand up to those drawn by a few of the world's most revered, unbiased thinkers like Lao-tzu, Confucius, Plato, Socrates, Aristotle, Seneca, Marcus Aurelius, Descartes, Emerson, Thoreau, James, Nietzsche, Hesse, Gibran, or the *thousands* of other respected voices from history for confirmation. I hope this book one day gives your own experiences, logic, and intuition such confirmation as well. Not that you need *any* authority other than yourself to stake your claim on life's unquestionable beauty and your immutable power.

I'm aware, of course, that putting words to truth can sometimes limit it. Due to this unavoidable language barrier, you're about to find subtle yet unavoidable *seeming* contradictions throughout this book.

Yet, I'd rather risk minor and temporary confusion to buck you from herd-like thinking, and to spark your own search for answers.

As you weigh and consider all I've written, call out the limitations and contradictions, but also find what resonates with your heart, aligns with your mind, and is evident in your life. When you discover an idea for which there's no such resonance, assuming enough of this book does, let it be an invitation for your own sense of personal responsibility to ask, "If this isn't the truth, *then what is*?"

If I convince you of nothing else, I will have succeeded if you grasp the immensity of your duty to ask that follow-up question for all things in life that trouble your heart, knowing that there is *always* a single answer to find and leverage for your own peace and happiness.

There are no other rules. There are no hidden agendas. And there are no unknown variables working against you. You truly do have dominion over all things, unmitigated by *anything* . . . except confusion over what the truth is.

Your "rock" this lifetime will come from understanding the most fundamental absolutes of our reality, which is what this chapter is about. Then, fear can be banished from your life and all good things added —peace, comfort, creativity, confidence, health, wealth, friendships, happiness, love, enlightenment, truly *all things.*

Which is exactly what I wish for you.

You're not here to earn your
    wings,
you're here because, in some long-forgotten realm,
    you **already** did.

You came **first.**
    Before the sun, the moon, and the stars.
You chose to be here.
    You're who **you** most wanted to be.

The reason you forget who you were
    before
        this **lifetime** began,
    is to more fully be who you **now** are.

"Reality" is not that you're **weak,**
　　　and dream of becoming strong;
poor, and dream of becoming rich;
　　　alone, and dream of having friends.
It's that you're strong, rich, and among friends—
　　　yet, at times, **dream** that you're not.

Thinking is life's only **variable.**
　　　Everything else was settled a long,
　　　　　long time ago.

In the most **basic** sense,
　　　life as we know it **began**
　　　　　when God set out, through us,
to think what has never been **thought.**

You are God's *only* chance to be **you**.
    To **see** what no one else will ever see,
to **hear** what no one else will ever hear,
      and to **think** and feel what no one else will
        ever think and **feel**.

You are more precious than you can possibly
    imagine.

You're already one of the most
    important
        people who will ever live.

The "**original** sin" was seeing the world of illusions
    and thinking they formed reality;
Adam biting into the **proverbial**, illusionary, apple
    as if it was real,
and thus falling from **grace**,
    falling from **truth**.

Every time we **react** to the world around us
    as though *it* were **reality**,
      we eat of the forbidden fruit.

If you **look** to time and space
for answers, direction, and **meaning**,
they'll rock your world in every which way.
Yet discover they look to *you* for answers,
direction, and meaning,
and you will **rock** the world.

The more you believe in **appearances**,
in the story told by your physical senses,
and see yourself as a **pawn** in the circumstances
you now find yourself in,
the **less** control you'll have over them.
By all means **enjoy** appearances,
just don't trust **them**.

It's not the "unseen" that's fiction,
but the **seen**.
What you can touch will one day disappear;
what you can feel will last **forever**.

The **truth** will not only set you free,
    it'll slay all dragons, banish all fears,
        heal what hurts, fill what's empty,
    clear what's confused, connect all dots,
lighten what's heavy, bring friends together,
        turn **dust** to gold,
            and raise the **sun**.

To **see** more and more of what we're missing
    fully explains the **evolution** of consciousness
        within time and space.

All deliberate change comes first from
    denying the logic that earlier
        gave you comfort.

Our **ability** to stop kidding ourselves
　　　is what brings about the **greatest**
breakthroughs, fastest comebacks,
　　　and happiest **feet**.

True love is a given, not an option;
　　　an **absolute**, not a variable.
Born of our divinity, not our humanity.
　　　Always **unconditional**.

Our **lives** are not about love,
　　　they're about our **adventures** into love.
Our adventures are the variable,
　　　not **love**.

Life is not just what you see,
   but what you've projected.
It's not just what you **feel**,
   but what you've decided.
It's **not** just what you've experienced,
   but how you've remembered it.
It's not just **what** you've forged,
   but what you've allowed.
And it's not just who's appeared,
   but who you've **summoned.**

One of the greatest paradoxes
   of your physical senses is that
      they actually show you what you believe,
as much as what you **perceive**—
   fortunately, the former is easier to change.

Instead of **running** from something scary,
   it's easier to learn not to be **scared** of it.

It's impossible to be scared when you **dwell** in truth.

Usually, **loving** more is easier than
      fearing less and gets **better** results.

You can only be afraid,
      when you pretend you're not in control.
Lonely, when you stop doing **things.**
      Bored, when you stop following your heart.
And overwhelmed, when you think
      the **illusions** are real.

The believed-in **myth** that you might somehow
      lose or become less is what makes
            life an adventure.

Fear goes away when you remember:
    First, you're a spiritual being.
And, second, nothing can ever be
    lost or taken from a spiritual being
        that cannot be re-created.

Sometimes it takes being pressed with darkness
    before you begin to seek the light.

Life does not happen to you.
    You happen to life.

While you'll often hear that change
    is life's only constant,
        the only thing really changing
            is you and what you understand.

Time and space are simply
measures of self-awareness.

For those whose thoughts are free,
so is everything else.
Whether or not they know it.

Whatever you want,
you deserve.

All forms of separation—
disconnects, divides, illnesses, partings,
breakups, and good-byes
—are temporary.

You are forever.

If speaking to a spiritual novice
      during the **earliest** days of human evolution,
you might explain God, metaphorically,
   as if "He" were angry, testing, and judgmental.
To someone a bit more savvy, during **easier** times,
    you might explain God, metaphorically, as if
"She" were always loving, nurturing,
      and forever conspiring on your behalf.
And to someone on the verge of total enlightenment,
    during the **latter** days of human evolution,
you might explain God by asking them
     to turn up the **music,**
        take off their **shoes,**
walk in the **grass,** unleash the dog,
   free the canary, catch a breeze,
      ride upon a wave, dream upon a star,
      dance
        every day,
get up early, take a nap, stay out late,
     eat chocolate, **feel** the **love,**
       give stuff **away,** earn it back,
    give some more,
      and **laugh.**

Heaven is everywhere, **always**, at once.
Hell is **not** knowing it.

Find the good in *every* circumstance. It's always there.

Behold God, **everywhere**, always, now.
There's no devil, nor does evil exist
of its own device.

Evil is simply ignorance in human **thought**,
misdiagnosed.

While there will be no such thing
as a "Judgment Day,"
        there are **consequences.**
And the consequences of misunderstanding life's truths
        are **likely** to include poor behavior,
repeating cycles, and, possibly, a truly harrowing
        adventure through time and space . . .
until your thinking aligns with **truth.**
        Which will only ever lie
                a few new **thoughts** away.

No matter how long you ignore **life's** magic
        or unwittingly swim against its current,
the **instant** you stop struggling
        you'll be back in the flow,
the prodigal child returned home,
        inheritance fully **restored.**

There are only **three** things you need
to know about **angels**:
1. They're real.
    2. Some exist to serve you.
        3. They can do the most when you **ask**
        them for help.

Just because you're a
    supernatural, unstoppable,
        creator doesn't mean you can't have
    friends on your team who **help** you out
from time to time.

Avoid gray areas.
    Therein, the **pathway** to safety and comfort
is guarded by the unreliable half-truths of
    "maybe," "sometimes," and "I don't know."
Life is absolute and its principles are **exacting.**
    In all things, there is *a* truth.

See everything through **truth's** light
    and you'll never know sadness, lack, or limits.
You'll see that you are safe. Bathed in **love.**
    Surrounded by admirers in both
        the physical and spiritual realms.
You'll see only beauty, perfection, and **meaning.**
    And you'll realize that just as the stark
contrasts of time and space may seem to imprison you,
    within them lies their own
        infinite possibilities.

Nothing will free you more than the **truth**
    and nothing will hold you back more
        than not **knowing** it.

If you **ever** get curious and wonder
    who you were meant to be,
look in the mirror and **smile.**

Your life's **purpose** is far more
    a function of being yourself,
than making clever **choices.**

Feeling lost does not **mean** you are.

All that you **need,** to have all that you want,
    lies inside of you right **now.**

While the notions of purpose, meanings,
    and destinies may **challenge** you,
one idea you can always be clear on is that the mind
    that spun the **cosmos** together
clearly has wishes and dreams all its own
    . . . that obviously included you.

    All is **supremely** well.

There is no choice you will ever make that might
limit you as much as you may fear.

Busy yourself doing what you most want,
among the possibly skimpy choices
you'll **sometimes** have,
and in no time you'll find that
your purpose has found you.

What's most important is that you're here.
A million times less important is
what you do here, when, **where,** and with whom.

You are not on earth to make things happen . . .
to spread the love . . . to make it a better place
or to learn acceptance of the things you cannot change.
You are not on earth to find your soulmate
or your **purpose**
. . . To put the needs of others before your own.
And you are most certainly not on earth to suffer,
pay penance, be tested, or **judged** . . .
. . . you are here because in your loftiest
state of being,
perched high above the wonderment,
at the **pinnacle** of your glory,
you wondered what it would be like,
even fleetingly, to believe in limits.
And when you can **grasp** this
from within the illusions,
you will also grasp how **unlimited** you truly are.

There are really only two conditions
of the human **experience:**
Very, very happy,
or, about to become very, very **happy.**

"Your happiness" is the ultimate answer to
every "WHY?" you could ever ask God.

Forever has only just begun.
Slow never fails to arrive.
And, happy always lasts longer than sad.

Time truly is on your side.

Happiness doesn't mean you've settled for less;
it means you're ready for more.

Some people are happiest when they're unhappy.
Let them be happy.

If you ever want to find a life partner,
    live in **greater** prosperity, be more productive,
foster peace on earth, or improve your health,
    if you can "be happy now," ahead of time,
before these things have **arrived,**
    then these things will arrive even faster.

Happiness isn't a crop you harvest when
    your dreams come **true.**
It's the fertilizer that makes them come true faster.
    It's also what opens the floodgates,
        beats your heart, finds true love,
            feeds your mind, and **frees** your soul.

The **wiser** you are, the easier life gets.
    But then, the happier you are,
the less you need easy.

By all means, seek to change the things you don't
like and to manifest the things you do,
just don't put off your **happiness** for either.

Happiness is the **one** option you'll always have
that no one can deny **you**.

The Law of Happy states:
However happy you've ever been,
you will one **day** be happier.

The **path** to enlightenment is not a path at all,
but a metaphor for the **time** it takes to live in joy,
no matter **what**.

When the world seems hard and clarity is elusive,
    you might refresh **your** thinking by reframing
time and space as the kindergarten of the Universe,
    not its Harvard.

Rising suns and babbling brooks.
    Tropical forests and sleeping meadows.
Modern marvels and scientific breakthroughs.
    Exciting discoveries and **limitless** frontiers.
Devoted friends and caring strangers.
    Lives and **loves** and souls to hold so close,
      your **heart** could burst . . .

While there may, at times, seem to be a lot of
    "real estate" between **where** you are
and where you dream of being,
    the road runs straight **through** paradise.

30

It's not that you have to wait
    for your dreams to come true,
but that you **get** to—
    in a magical world where **love** abounds,
in the palm of God's **hand,**
    until your brief turn in **space** is over.

The **reason** butterflies float, fireflies light,
    comets fall, trees grow, cats purr, and tails wag
is because each is **reflecting** something in you,
    at the very moment of perception,
disguised by the elements, captured in time,
    to remind you of your sublime **divinity.**

If you ever find yourself driving down
    the motorway of **life,**
        looking for an exit that says "Easy Street" . . .
      consider, that's **probably**
        where we got on,
following a sign that said, "Paradise, this way.
    Road Under Construction.
      Watch out for lightworkers,
        invisible beliefs, and runaway dogma.
      No **stopping.**"

The **great** perfection of living a lifetime
    within a world of **illusions**
lies in the fact that no matter what happens next,
    you'll be richer for it.

People, when given a chance, smile,
      skip, and dance.
    They create, play, and laugh.
They care, share, and **love.**

The ones who don't, haven't yet **realized** that
    chances are something you give to yourself.

No **matter** your path,
    you will one day see that the **good**
        and the beautiful
    wildly **exceeded** the bad and the ugly.

Should you ever overhear someone say
    they're only human,
remind them it's just for a **short** while, that before
    long they'll be able to see their wings again,
speak in tongues, and blaze trails throughout
    eternity upon chariots of fire.

The **dead** do have their day,
    and they all live beyond it.
No one really dies.

To the **naked** eye death appears random.
  To the spiritually inclined it appears
    ordained.

Life is so magnificent that once you pass
    from this plane, even your times of sorrow,
fear, frustration, anger, confusion, and loneliness
    will be dearly missed.

But you'll **smile** when you find them as carefully
    set jewels in your crown of **compassion.**

You'll cry **happy** tears as the veils of time fall away
    revealing that each moment of the **life** you
just lived is still **unfolding.**

And you'll laugh when you **realize** this all
    could have been u**nderstood** when you were
who you now **are.**

34

The odd thing about the often long and lonely path
of life is that when you get to the end
of it and look back,
you'll find that it was neither.

Do not fear that at the end of your life,
you will somehow disappear back into God
the way a cube of sugar dissolves into a hot drink,
for even now you live your life inside of God,
while at the same time maintaining your own
radiant essence and glorious identity.

It's good to remember that all roads lead "home."
It's better to realize that you never really left.

Given the world's uncertainty
    about what happens at death,
it's easy to imagine that the main thing those who've
    "passed"would like to tell those who haven't is
that once you get over the shock of your safe arrival—
    completely intact, cool as ever,
        bathed in love—
what you'll miss most about Earth
    is the beguiling romance of uncertainty.

Not that you won't also miss windy mornings,
        starry skies, and old trees; bare feet,
          barking dogs, and beige;
beetles, strawberries, and doorbells;
    coffee, blue jeans,
        and falling leaves.

2

how
"things"
happen:

the logistics of magic & miracles

I remember hearing your heart beat for the first time, months before you were born. A heartbeat where earlier there'd been none. It was like hearing spirit knock on a door that would eventually open to time and space. "Miracle" fails to adequately describe the transformation of spirit into flesh.

And ever since, your presence and growth has ushered before us a procession of magical moments. Truly, if human beings only knew of how many miracles they performed every day, just by being here, nothing else in our lives would ever again overwhelm us, frighten us, or seem impossible.

Another one of my life's big "Aha!" moments, was finding that miracles need not bend the physical laws of the universe to blow our minds or leave us speechless. Most don't. And as you learn to create consciously, you'll actually begin to notice, with hindsight, that most of your extraordinary accomplishments will occur through an implausible, though wholly ordinary, series of events.

For example, dreaming of Prince Charming (no hurry, please), when followed with consistent, thoughtful action, unclouded with misunderstandings and contradictions, *will* lead to meeting Prince Charming . . . although through a seemingly natural sequence of "routine" events, that "coincidentally" lined up, each absolutely crucial and exquisitely timed, *that never would have occurred without the initial dream*. This is because all manifestations begin with a desired *end result*, which then *attracts* the right ideas, circumstances, and people onto your path. Ultimately creating a life that resembles, *or surpasses*, whatever you were originally thinking about.

Most miracles remain invisible and are unknown until long after they transpire. Yet you perform them all the time, we all do. Human beings are non-stop, can't-be-turned-off-even-if-we-wanted-to-be, natural-born creators. We are *matter manipulators* by way of our everyday thoughts, because these are the de facto *end results* that we end up believing in and acting on.

Of course, at first it doesn't seem possible that we could be "happening" to life in this way. Too many things we wish for never show up and too many things we never imagined do. You're sure to have as many objections and questions as I once did. But as you stay with it, insisting upon truth, opening heart and mind, you'll finally see the obvious:

- Thoughts become things, unless other thoughts of yours get in the way.

- When the unthought-of happens, it's always a stepping-stone in a journey to a farther destination *that you had thought of.*

- Shared manifestations, in a world of 7+ billion co-creators, like the weather or the economy, arise based on the participants' collective thoughts, confusions, and behaviors.

- Before this lifetime began, you knew the prevailing collective thoughts, and therefore the world's probabilities for war or peace, feast or famine, and other transformations or upheavals, as well as localized probabilities like how your parents might be challenged and how your other family members might live their lives. These either played into your life's private intentions or were irrelevant.

- It's usually "impossible" for a personal manifestation to violate core collective beliefs about the nature of reality, like the physical laws of the world. Were this to happen, it would tear the fabric of your collective life stage. Because of this, you can't turn charging lions into house cats. But your thoughts followed by action, like possessing an intense focus on survival and running for your life, might trigger a herd of passing zebras to distract those lions—which would be no less miraculous.

- While the collective may deny you certain freakish manifestations (like turning lions into kitties) and while you may temporarily give your power away to certain individuals, no one can ultimately keep you from manifesting more friends and laughter, health and healing, wealth and abundance, or living a happy, fulfilling life.

And it gets better.

A lot better.

Almost unimaginably better.

Your positive thoughts are far more likely to become "things" than your negative ones.

If this sounds over the top, consider: Haven't you smiled more than you've frowned? Laughed more than you've cried? Had clarity more than confusion? Friends more than enemies? Health more than sickness? Money more than being in the red? And in all such comparison, aren't the differences usually by GIGANTIC proportions? Can you then begin to see that life is not some 50/50 roll of the dice? That it's "*not* fair"? That nothing from your past can prevent you from thinking and thus creating anew?

Positive thoughts *are* in alignment with the beauty and power that brought us here. Thinking "positive" is going with the flow, instead of resisting it. That's why it has more power. Even part-time positivity can over-rule nearly full-time negativity, so long as it exists both in thought and deed.

You are not expected to become a miracle worker. You already are one. Should spirit move you to explore this further, however, I urge you to begin noticing exactly how you've been "accidentally" doing what you do, and to start doing it deliberately, consciously, and with abandon. The lessons in this chapter will get you grounded in understanding the logistics of creation, opportunity, moving beyond limits, and your power over life's illusions. I'll take these concepts further in chapter 4 with lessons on how to apply them.

Fortify what you learn here with the evidence that's now everywhere in your life. We're literally built to thrive. *You're built to thrive.* It's our default setting *in absolutely all regards.* As wildly successful as the human race has been so far, *it's been so in spite of our profound naivetes—thinking that God is angry or that we're here by accident!* Can you imagine the scale of breakthroughs we'll experience once everyone sees the obvious, releases fear, and engages their power? This is where we're headed, and that day swiftly approaches.

I want it for you now.

No **matter** what you may go after in life,
    getting what you want will always boil down to
        at least a little bit of **Divine** Intervention
           —your own.

The **speed** with which any dream may be realized
    is always a function of how small
        the miracles have to be in order not to
freak out the **dreamer.**

The **difference** between "have" and "have-not"
    is always down to imagination.

There are **three** things that will
    always evade your physical senses:
trees growing, the earth spinning,
    and dreams coming **true**.
Never assume these things aren't happening
    based upon what you see.

Detours, challenges, and crises are **simply** cover for
    miracles that have no other way of reaching you.

Don't let the miracles that have not transpired yet,
    blind you to those that have.

Your **dreams** are what the Universe
    has dreamed for **you**.

Most miracles aren't obvious
    until long after they happen,
which likely **means** that in your **life**,
    as you read these words,
some big ones have recently happened
    that will soon **change** everything.

At **all** times, far more is happening on your behalf
    than your physical **senses** will ever reveal.

While **knowledge** is indeed power,
    very little must be known
to dream, act, manifest, and be **happy.**

Wanting more is just the first sign of many
that you're going to get it.

"**Thoughts** become things"
explains where you fit into
the equation of reality **creation**.
As a *creator*
yourself.

What **mortals** don't realize is that
for every thought they think
the **physical** world is changed.
Not knowing this is the main thing
that makes us mortal.

Nothing will change your life
　　as much as
　　　　changing your **mind.**

Until you dream, there isn't a mold.
　　Until you speak, there isn't a promise.
And until you move, there isn't a **path.**
　　Yet do these things,
　　　　and you'll rearrange
　　　　　　the stars that shine on your **life.**

Divine Intelligence did not create
the physical universe by studying quarks,
drawing schematics, or painting butterflies.

It began by **imagining** the desired end result:
the vastness, the harmony,
the symbiotic relationships,
a stage to play out our lessons,
and in an instant, Big Bang.

Everything necessary for life as we know it,
including the supporting math, sciences,
and physical laws of the universe,
was spontaneously created
and forced into place
by the desired end result *that required such.*

Your **chosen** "end results" will do the same,
forcing the details, circumstances, people,
serendipities, accidents, and coincidences
that will ultimately bring about
the **manifestation**
of your earlier thoughts.

Your net worth will depend mostly
on your net thoughts.

The **concepts** of destiny, fate, luck, coincidences,
and accidents are all contrary or subordinate to
the inviolate **principle** of *thoughts becoming things,*
and will therefore always fail to fully explain
the life that you lead.

Ancient spiritual contracts
of the kind you will no doubt read of,
do indeed exist and provide a framework
for every **facet** of the life you'll lead.
However, they're rewritten every dawn,
perpetually updated as **each** day unfolds,
and all stipulate they're to become null and void
in the **event** they might ever limit you.

Karma is a phenomenon, not a law,
    that contributes to the manifestation
      of your life and circumstances
    reflective of your focus, behavior, and beliefs.

If your **focus,** behavior, and beliefs are
    negative or positive, generous or stingy,
you will give and receive accordingly;
    what goes around will **indeed** come around.

But change your focus, behavior, and beliefs
    and you'll immediately begin
      to change your **experiences,**
    regardless of any karmic "score."

Nothing that's **happened** in your past
    can take from your present power
      to choose new thoughts,
        create a new life,
          and be **happy.**

Our **beliefs** are almighty
    because they inspire or shut down our thinking,
and it's the thoughts **our** beliefs encourage
    or shut down that can or can't then **become**
the things and events of our **lives.**

While your beliefs will mostly be invisible,
    what they manifest will appear everywhere
        in your **life.**
You simply need to look at those areas that displease you
    to find where you might begin with some
introspection, probing, and **rethinking.**

One way to defeat invisible, limiting beliefs
   is to dream *and move* toward a life so grand
that the only way those new thoughts
   could become things is if any beliefs in their
   way were obliterated.
      And so they shall be.

Your beliefs are only invisible when you
   live within their limits.
Better to reach, stretch, and dream big.

Just because you might not know what your
   limiting beliefs are,
you can always know the kinds of empowering
   beliefs you'd like to possess.
Write these down. Get used to them.
   See their validity. And then,
one decision at a time, one day at a time,
   choose to behave with the mind
   of the highest within you.
Until that's all there is.

Your **words** are your thoughts
        that will become things the soonest—
    let them be of what you like and love.
What you care about and **cherish**.
        What serves you and makes you happy.
    What gives you wings and makes your heart sing.
        What makes you **dream**.
And very little else.

A **focus** on undesirable circumstances
        will usually extend and **multiply**
            those circumstances.

When you **talk** about "what is" or "what was,"
        even if just explaining to a friendly ear,
    you risk projecting **more** of the same
        into your future.

When you truly understand how **life** works,
   you'll rarely, if ever, say things like,
"It's hard,"
      "It's not working," or
         "Something's wrong with me."

Instead, you'll start saying things like,
      "I'll find the time for that."
         "Good thing I'm rich."
or "I can't take a bad picture."

The **emotional** highs and lows
   of any given day reveal **exactly**
what you've been telling yourself on that **day.**

The **mason,** disappointed with the form of fresh
concrete, does not try to **reshape** it;
she starts over.

Often, having what you want
is a function of mentally letting **go**
of what you have.

Just because you're not being judged,
doesn't mean you live in a world that's
neutral to your existence.
You are loved, supported,
and inclined to succeed.

Your **positive** thoughts are at least 10,000 times
more powerful than your negative thoughts.

Don't **worry** that you worry.
Even the fewest positive thoughts,
words, and steps taken, **every** day,
can turn any tide and right any ship.

Self-correcting, rebounding, and healing
are both in your nature
and **entirely** normal.

The **best** hope one has for thriving
    among the seen, the known, and the manifested
comes from playing off the **unseen,**
    the unknown, and the not yet manifested.

There's always more than one right answer,
    path, possibility, partner, nuance, or flavor—
so insist upon none,
    or you'll **exclude** all others.

It's not the day you have to manage,
    but the **moment.**
It's not the dragon you have to slay,
    but the fear.
And it's not the path you have to **know,**
    but the destination.

The "Bermuda Triangle of Manifesting"
    contains 3 "things" you can never be assured
of successfully micromanaging:
    specific people behaving in *specific* ways,
        how a dream will come true,
            and unimportant details
(by the way, all details are unimportant).

The workaround is simple:
    imagine **abundance,** not a dollar amount,
        love without insisting upon **who,**
            and a **rocking** *life,*
not just bells, whistles, and bling.

To **safeguard** that you're not in
    the Bermuda Triangle of Manifesting,
punctuate the end of each expressed desire with
    "or better."

To insist upon whos, hows, wheres, and minutiae
is to limit an otherwise unlimited Universe.

Dwell upon the WOWs, not the hows.

The problem with compromising,
economizing, and settling for less,
is that these results are no easier to manifest
than their fuller counterparts.

Life's magic has to work just as hard
whether the bar's been lowered or raised.

Don't be afraid to go where you've never gone
and do what you've never done,
because both are necessary
to have what you've never had
and to be who you've never been.

It's not the **dazzling** voice that makes a singer.
Or clever stories that make a writer.
And it's not piles of money that make a tycoon.
It's having a **dream**
and wanting to live it so **greatly**
that you'd rather move with it and "fail"
than succeed in another realm.

When the fear of **things** staying the same
exceeds the fear of failure,
things **happen**.

A **dream** not followed by consistent action,
points either to **thoughts** of contradiction
or misunderstandings.

Hoping, **wishing,** and praying
shouldn't ever be confused
with **doing.**

You were not **born** to wait.
You were born to **create.**

It **only** takes one second in time
for everything to **fantastically**
change for the better,
and you're far more likely to have one such second
by *actively living* as many as you can.

Being **excited** about the truth
   is never enough to change your life.
You must physically live the **truth.**

You don't have to do "it" **right,**
   you just have to **do** "it."

The **next** step on your path to living the life
   of your wildest dreams
      will rarely lie behind doors marked
         "WOW," "SEXY," or "GLAMOROUS."

Life's **magic** works through you.
    Not beside you. Not around you.
Not for you. Not instead of you.
       Through **you.**

In life, it's as if we each must choose
    from countless **doorways,**
        all leading to new and different hallways.
So we **wonder** and think, calculate and stress,
    over whether or not we'll knock on the "right" one.
But what we can't yet see is that
    all of the **hallways** beyond all of the doorways
eventually lead to the same great room,
    in the same great house,
       at the same great party.

Although there are rare exceptions,
    the **more** you do,
        the more will be **done** for you.

Taking massive action, on **massive** dreams,
    amid massive uncertainties,
        is pretty much where anyone who's ever done
anything massive had to **start.**
    And then things got way easier.

At any **point** in your life,
    the greater the uncertainties you face,
the greater your **chances** of hitting a major,
    life-changing "home run."

Changing what you have
    comes from changing who you are,
which comes from changing what you **think,**
    which comes from changing what you believe,
which are led by **desire** and action.

Simply **wanting** something reinforces the belief
    that you don't have what you want,
perpetuating that lack.
    Instead, name what you don't yet have by giving
thanks in advance for having received it,
    as if you **already** had.

When you **give** thanks for what you already have,
    the corresponding **manifestation**
        will expand and increase what you have.
When you give **thanks** for what you don't have,
    as if you already had it,
        the corresponding manifestation will **attract**
        and create it into your life.

Prayers that lack conviction, confidence,
and end in question marks like,
"Can I? May I? Will I?"
get answers like, "Sure! You bet! No question!"
They don't get results.
Which is fine, unless you wanted results.
Don't ask. Give thanks.

Giving heartfelt thanks for the good fortunes
that befall others—no matter who they are
—will help yield similar good fortunes for you.

It's not wanting that unlocks wheels, parts seas,
and changes everything.
It's expecting so greatly
that you begin preparing
and thanking in advance.

What you give, will be given to **you**.

To **find** out how much you've truly been blessed,
    in terms of love, time, **energy,**
or any other quality, substance,
    or dispensation, give of them.
Then you'll know what **boundless** really means.

Giving demonstrates a belief you are provided for.
    It's an act of **faith**
        that implies you will remain whole,
that what you gave will come back to you,
    and that **love** is what matters most.

And when you believe these things
    they'll become your reality, and abundance will
        be **showered** upon you
as if the **heavens** had opened up.

It's always **better** to give too much, pay too much,
 and love too much than not enough,
especially when you understand
 it all comes **back** anyway.

Once **enlightened,** you can do less and have more.
 But . . . once enlightened,
  who would want to do less
when you finally **realize** the world spins
 in your very hand, your thoughts become things,
  and you can have, do, or be
   anything you want
when you **simply** show up, have fun,
 and keep busy?

Unofficially, I'd say that the number-one cause
    of loneliness is not a lack of friends,
            but a lack of keeping busy.
And that nine out of ten times the solution to
    every crisis, challenge, or problem
            —in relationships, careers, or otherwise
            —is to get busy.

One out of ten times . . . the solution will be to
    first get quiet, and then get busy.

Little is more impressive,
    inspirational, or sexy than watching
someone in the throes of action,
    driven by purpose, oblivious to all but their aim.
And anyone, including you, can be that person,
    on any day you choose.

It's easier to fall in love,
    and to be fallen in love with,
when you're busy.

The busier you are the faster time flies,
    the less you worry,
        the more friends you have,
the farther you travel, the richer you become,
    the quicker you rebound,
        and the happier you feel.

Plus, chances of being in the right place
    at the right time increase exponentially.
Not just for the improved odds,
    but the improved faith it demonstrates.

You can only ever do what you can,
    with what you have, from where you are.
Yet by design,
        it'll always be **enough.**

Usually, the best way to find the yellow brick road
    of your **life** is to start out on the dusty dirt one.
And to let yourself become so preoccupied
    in making the **best** of it, having **fun,**
        and challenging yourself
that you actually stop paying **attention** to the path.

Until, **one** day, not too long after you began,
    with a new best friend, feeling awesome
and a teeny tiny bit taller,
    looking down at your **path**
        you'll **notice** that it's "24 karats."

Then you'll **wonder** for a long time,
    probably as you sip on an exotic fruit drink,
        on what day the transformation
            actually took place

You **may** not be able to take "it" with you
at the end of your **life,**
but whatsoever you may do, be,
or have in **time** and space
awaits you on the **other** side.

The **path** to enlightenment
usually includes many stages.
Most commonly, it begins with
festering misunderstandings that lead to pain,
the pain then leads to growth,
growth leads to **clarity,**
clarity leads to fun,
fun leads to joy,
and joy leads to true **illumination**.

Whenever possible, and it usually is,
I recommend skipping to the **fun** part.

3

learning from

all

that hurts

I bet it's a beautiful day when you read this. Not necessarily sunshiny and breezy, or even daylight, but sparkling with possibilities and laden with potential. They all are.

Just three years ago, part of my morning ritual, after changing and feeding you breakfast, was to take a short walk, carrying you past a few houses and back. In the winter I'd swaddle you in a blanket, and on warmer days leave your bare arms and legs to the morning's breeze.

You'd never fail to hold your head high, eyes wide, silently periscoping as I chronicled all I saw . . . from the rising sun, to overhead birds plying the sky, waving neighbors headed off to work, a snail crossing the sidewalk in front of us, peppered with flowery descriptions, observing and declaring that it was, yet another, *"Beautiful day!"*

By the time you were walking and talking, age three, some mornings, at the first sign of sunrise, you'd creep into our room and timidly ask with a sleep-strained voice, "Daddy . . . is . . . it . . . a bea-u-ti-ful day? Is it a bea-u-ti-ful day, Daddy?" And then as you heard us stir, gaining in tempo and excitement, you'd continue, *"Is it a beautiful day?! Is it a beautiful day?! Is it a beautiful day?!"* Not really questioning the day's beauty, but wanting to know if it was, in fact, a *new* day—confident, I choose to believe, in your early wisdom, that all days are beautiful.

Of course, *everything* that happens within every moment of any day is born of meaning, order, and love—the epitome of beauty. Even though sometimes, to the physical senses, things might appear to be anything but. That such seeming contradictions unexpectedly crop up, however, will not mean that you aren't solely creating your life nor will it mean that God is serving up "tests." We are our own teachers and there are no tests, as you'll soon read.

This is the trickiest chapter, because what's to be shared can seem naïve, negative, or just plain offensive. But consider, if you're beginning to understand that you live a life of your own creation, couched in love, then just maybe, the more any of these carefully vetted chapter lessons sting or offend, the more you have to learn. Life's perfection isn't part-time. It's all the time. And when we suffer it's always because *we've* missed something, not because we've found a flaw in the world. Yes, there's ugliness, but it's never pointless. Find the point and you'll close in on the healing; see the healing and you'll find love.

Accepting Responsibility

Coming to terms with your supernatural power, means accepting your supernatural responsibilities. To live full throttle, you must accept responsibility for *everything* that has ever happened to you. Including your birth and those experiences that were seemingly thrust upon you. If Prince Charming is not who you thought he'd be, move on, but also try to understand your beliefs about men and relationships that led you to define, want and choose him as you once did.

At first, this may seem unfair, to say the least. Yet life is an adventure into possibilities and experimentation. Everyone choosing to be alive at this early stage of our civilization's development made this choice knowing that ugly things might happen. Made possible, in part, by our own misunderstandings, at a time when unintentional manifestations would be the norm. But we also knew that we'd be surrounded by beauty and possibilities, in a world sustained by love. That we'd be able to change most circumstances we found displeasing. We also knew we'd "return home" unscathed, even greater for the experience, eternity still calling, no matter what had just happened in the fleeting, imaginary illusions of time and space.

By claiming responsibility for all things in your life, you reclaim your power. You no longer believe *that others, fate, or God decides what happens to you.* You cease being a victim. You begin living on your terms.

Life Lessons

All dreams come with built-in challenges. If not, you'd already have what you want and there'd be no dream. One does not exist without the other, but our challenges only reveal themselves once we start moving toward our dreams. For example, wanting your dream job, but finding it requires public speaking. Moving in with Romeo, to discover *he* wasn't quite ready. Wanting to write a book, then learning what that demands. Your dreams are part of how you will one day become the person you know you can be; they call you down a path upon which you learn "the price" you must pay for their realization. If you like, you can think of them as tests you must pass, but not given by God— created instead from the collision and juxtaposition of your old thoughts (that led to today) and your new ones (that will make your dreams come true).

With more critical thinking you'll see your challenges show you where your thoughts and beliefs need clarity. They are hurdles that perfectly match your evolution at the exact moment you're ready to take the next step. *This is how it works.* Your dreams aren't random, they're custom fitted (by you) to take you on a journey that will teach what *you* wanted to learn—maybe not consciously, but effectively. That's the whole point: your dreams lie beyond your reach, *so that you will reach!*

How I *desperately* wish that you'd never suffer the pain of a broken heart—never know what it is to be slighted, feel lost, unworthy, insufficient—the list of such agonies is endless. Yet when I reflect on my own life, I'm truly frightened by the thought of how much less I'd be today had such grievances been shielded from me, denying me the spiritual insights and emotional wisdom that have come from my own times of defeat, heartbreak, and humiliation. These scars have given my subsequent life quests traction and made possible achieving heights of love and confidence that earlier I couldn't even have imagined.

The emotional pains you'll inevitably encounter will hurt me every bit as much as they'll hurt you, but avoiding them is not the answer. Learning to rebound, grow, and flourish despite them is—which I hope to help you with through the following lessons. This chapter is about reframing how you view setbacks and problems, helping you to leverage the gifts that come from adversity, because no trifling of the past, no matter how great, can tarnish the brilliance of eternity.

Love you, mean it.

Always,
    the thing that didn't work out for your very,
        very best
. . . really did.

You didn't choose this **lifetime**
    thinking it would be without challenges.
You chose it, in large part,
    for the challenges you'd likely have.

When something troubling, difficult,
    or painful happens,
look to see what it makes **possible**,
    that wouldn't have otherwise been possible,
and you'll find at least part of its reason for happening.

The path to enlightenment must include:
Accepting full responsibility
for your own happiness. And . . .
Accepting full responsibility
for your own *unhappiness*.

It's one kind of **victory** to slay a beast,
move a mountain, and cross a chasm;
it's another kind **altogether**
to realize that the beast,
the mountain, and the chasm
were of your own design.

If not for your **challenges**, problems, and issues,
how else would you know there are still
a few things you **misunderstand**?

Every "no" **means** "not yet."
　　Every setback means "there's something **better.**"
Every loss means "even more is on the way."
　　And every disappointment, "pucker up, buttercup."

It's not just that when one **door** closes,
　　another door opens.
When one door closes, choirs burst into chorus,
　　orchestras orchestrate, bugles bugle, pigs fly,
and 10,000 new doors **open.**

It's no one's **responsibility** to tell you
　　what your "issues" are,
and contrary to popular thinking, most will not.
　　Which pretty much means there'll only be
one person you can trust in such matters.

Where you are is never **who** you are.

You're not **alive** to face hurdle after hurdle;
it's not as if, should you master your issues today,
more will be added tomorrow.
While there'll always be more to learn,
as you become wiser you'll find
you have fewer challenges,
which are each quite manageable,
feeling more like **opportunities**
than burdens.

The only **real** problem you'll ever have
is thinking you have a problem.

When you prepare for adversity,
you build not a bridge to retreat by,
but one for adversity to advance upon.

Once you **realize** that everything difficult you go
through—every scuffed knee, lost deal,
or broken heart—
will eventually play wildly in your favor,
you'll find it hard to complain
about **anything**.

Every **challenge is** an invitation
to a happier place than you even knew existed.

Setbacks, delays, and disappointments
are like steps in the mambo,
tango, and cha-cha.
If you studied the movements
without knowing the dance,
nothing would make sense.
But when you see the big picture—
poetry in motion.

If, ever in your life, suddenly and without warning,
  an event, person, or unexpected good news
changes **everything** for the better,
  it will mean chances are astronomically **high**
. . . that it will happen again.
    And again. And again.

Words like *blame, victim,* or *fault*
  should never be used in enlightened conversations—
instead try *creator, adventurer,* or heroine.

Wondering **how** else you could view life
    when you're experiencing emotional
      or physical pain
is a sign of **spiritual** maturity.
  Wondering how else you could view life
when things are already going really well
  is the sign of a **spiritual** rock star.

If you aren't constantly pushing yourself to grow,
    it'll mean you're **missing** something.
And that thing you're missing
    will eventually cause you to fall,
leading you to push yourself as you get back up,
    repeating itself until you understand
        what you were missing.
All of which can be avoided when,
    even though you think you aren't missing
anything at all, you continually **push** yourself.

You're not **meant** to bear that which you find
    unpleasant; you're meant to **change** it.

Anger is almost always a sign
    that you've been **quiet** for too long.
But instead of offering a solution,
    it closes the mind and cools the **heart**
when both are needed most.

Usually the person you're angry at
      has the most to teach you.

Not that they're **necessarily** right about
      whatever you're angry about.

It won't be your cake-for-breakfast,
      pajamas-in-the-afternoon,
        he-loves-me kind of times
you'll remember at the end of your life
      with the **greatest** fondness,
but your bounced-back, fears-faced,
      and I-love-him kind of times.

Setbacks are only devastating
      when you **think** they'll last forever.
They never do.

Sometimes you have to move away, to get closer.

Let go, to stake your claim.

Be still, to move forward.

Give, to receive.

Cry, to feel the joy.

Pretend, to make it **real**.

Fake it, before you make it.

And sometimes, you must first decide
to **feel** their love, to find it was there all along.

Exactly where you've been will make possible
exactly who you become.
And one day, no matter where you've been,
you'll wake up and feel so much joy for your life,
exactly as is,
that you wouldn't trade *anything* for your past,
exactly as it was . . .
nor exactly as it is on the day you read this.

The **biggest** misconception people have about the past
   is thinking it can detract from the rest of their lives.

To the contrary, the past only ever makes
   more things possible.

Although this might not make sense now,
   always consider, that at the deepest level,
all pain is self-inflicted.
   And when this does make sense,
      you'll find it's really **great** news.

Almost no one would ever choose an **adventure**
   if they knew they'd become hopelessly lost,
have their heart broken to pieces,
   or at times wish **they'd** never been born.
But absolutely everyone would choose any of those
   scenarios if they also knew that
because of the chaos they'd sooner find themselves,
   fall passionately in love,
      and live **happily** ever after.

The **only** way to find your way is to first be lost.
To make it big, start out small.
To **fall** in love, first feel none.
So, any such feelings of being lost, feeling small,
missing love, or the like should be seen as signs
that you've made a really big and daring "wish,"
and the manifestation process has **already** begun.

Of all the **joys** on earth, few compare to
the crowning glory of achieving against the odds,
succeeding in the face of peril,
or triumphing over adversity.
Yet in every such case, **without** exception,
the poor odds, peril, and adversity must come first.

Talking a lot about something that bothers you
is a pretty good sign
you've got something profoundly
liberating to learn.

That **which** curses you today will bless you tomorrow.
That is, if you come to believe in curses
and blessings
in a world where there are only **miracles.**

Said another way,
the more challenges you face on any given day,
the more happy **dancing**
and **high fives** will follow.

You don't have to know how you got yourself into
any mess to know how to **move** from it.

Just because you won't always physically see life's order,
especially during crises or when disappointed,
won't mean you can't always deduce
it **must** be there . . .
in absolutely insane wall-to-wall proportions.

The only **hint** you might receive
    that you've begun living
the greatest chapter of your life,
    is that it might start out **feeling** like the worst.

Admit, confess, and atone before you have to,
    because one day, you'll have to.
And on that day you'll realize it would have been far better
    to act and call out your **naiveté,**
than wait for the ambush.

Sadness, fear, and despair are less conditions
    than they are **decisions**—
to see yourself as less than you really are.

When you **feel** happy, especially really happy,
   it'll seem that you've always been happy
      and that you'll **always** be happy.

Which is just as true when you feel really sad,
   lonely, depressed, broke, sick, or scared.

Which means how you **choose** to feel on any given
   day will recharacterize how you feel
      about your entire life.

Disappointments have little to do with circumstance
   and **everything** to do with perspective.

You can **change** how you feel
   in the twinkling of an eye
if you just change what you view as important.

For whatever bothers you,
    not that it shouldn't,
know that YOU are the reason
    it bothers you.

Practice seeing everything with spiritual eyes,
    and you'll find
. . . no predicament that can't
    be turned into an advantage,
        . . . no foe who can't become a friend, and
            . . . no burden that can't give you wings.

The reason others might think they need you
    is because they won't yet believe they already
have all that it takes to have all that they want.
    So they pretend you hold the key.

And, maybe, sometimes, you might be tempted
    to think the same about someone else.

While in the **pursuit** of a grand and wonderful dream,
should you suddenly round a bend and see before you
an enormous uncharted mountain with
towering cliffs, **jagged** rocks,
and seemingly impenetrable walls,
consider it a sign that your dream is far more
worthwhile than you had previously imagined.

When fear **speaks,** it's almost always wrong.
Unless you're being chased by **wildebeests.**
And when love speaks, it's almost always right.
And usually **bouncy.**

However wrong fear is, it often appears when you're in
exactly the right place, at exactly the right time,
doing exactly what you "should" be doing
to learn the most.

Next time you meet fear, ask,
"How **might** I use you and what may I learn?"

Look to what you're afraid of
to learn where you can grow.

Actually, **life's** lions and tigers and bears
are really just angels and fairies and unicorns
that followed you here, in disguise, from worlds beyond,
agreeing to poke, unnerve, and awaken you
whenever you forget
that you're **dreaming.**

When you see **things** that pain you, sadden you,
or make your heart ache, remember,
you're not **seeing** all.

If you think **deeply** enough upon those things
    that cause you great suffering and consternation,
you'll ultimately find great **joy** and illumination.

It really is an **itty-bitty** world we live on.
    And if you can maintain this **perspective**,
you'll be pleasantly surprised by how
    your challenges shrink.

The **first** step you might take
    toward changing unpleasant circumstances . . .
is to stop **dwelling** upon those circumstances.

The best **remedy** for dealing with a troubling past
    is living in the **present.**

Not on your "worst day," **during** your lowest ebb,
nor through your most challenging circumstances
will you fail to **rebound**
to higher heights than before.

If ever you find yourself sitting in the darkness,
and then **decide** you want to sit in the light,
consider, your first few steps must be in the darkness.

Letting **go** is always easier than holding on.
And it's how **new** stuff can find you faster.

It's **easier** to let go of the past once you realize that
no matter how differently things might have gone,
you still couldn't be more **loved** than you now are,
nor could you have more to look forward to.

Whenever there's a **genuine** commitment,
    no matter what direction you choose,
all of life's elements will align
    to gain you an advantage, stack the deck, and
prepare one and all for some serious legend making.

The **greater** the emotional pain,
    the greater the desire had been to **learn** the most.

Look to what's beautiful for truth.
    And to what hurts for its **beauty**.

Whenever **feeling** confused, conflicted,
    or bored by life, seek a higher perspective.
Because feeling confused, conflicted, or bored
    means **there** is one.

No matter how **things** may ever seem,
    friends are always near and love is always **present**.

Nothing is ever lost.
    Not time;
    for what seems to have passed
        lives on in the wisdom of future decisions.
Not money;
    for what seems to have been spent
        was only **invested**.
And not love;
    for what seems to have vanished
        has **only** moved so close you must look
within your heart to find it.

There is no harm, misstep, violation,
    or disaster that cannot be amended,
balanced, corrected, or **fixed**.

Sometimes, when it seems your wings have suddenly
and unexpectedly been clipped,
maybe, just maybe, there's **more** to learn
by **staying** where you are.

Taking **responsibility** *doesn't mean*
you have to understand
the nuances of your **role**
in **bringing** about painful events,
other than acknowledging you had a role.
Nor does it mean condoning
past or present violations
or that you shouldn't defend yourself,
speak up, protest, be heard,
press **charges**, file suit,
or warn others.

Neither **does** it mean you're to blame or are at fault.

You're an ancient gladiator of love and joy who,
    when choosing this lifetime, *knew what you were doing.*
Can you **imagine**, then,
    considering your magnificence and zest for life,
you might **not** want to live every adventure on
    "easy street"?
    That on occasion, if not as a rule,
you might *want to* be **challenged?**

That you might sometimes choose to be in harm's way
    to spare others the pain?

That you might want to see what
    you're **truly** capable of achieving and enduring?
How deeply you might love and be loved?

    All under a variety of **circumstances?**

It's **often** from a sense of discontent,
    feelings of incompleteness,
        or even a **twinge** of true unhappiness,
that the seeds of great accomplishment
    and transformation are sown.

The more from your past that you accept
responsibility for, **including** absolutely,
positively everything,
the more in your future you'll have the power to
change, including absolutely,
positively **everything**.

Should you ever feel a bit bummed out
and not know why
. . . or catch yourself looking back over your shoulder,
wondering . . . or sometimes **asking**,
What's taking so long? . . . understand,
this is typical of all spiritual **overachievers**.

The **easiest** way to avoid letdowns
     and disappointments
   is never tricking yourself into **thinking**
that your happiness is dependent upon
    the things and events of time and **space**.

   Which is not to imply you can't change both.

Emotional pains are just truth
    knocking upon a door
       that's been **closed** too long.

Every story has a **happy** ending if you believe in
    endings—either in this lifetime or thereafter.
And this alone, when factoring in all of **life's**
    splendors, will make any fleeting pain and sorrow
totally and unquestionably **"worth it."**

The thing that makes the darkest of times bearable,
  is **remembering** that life as you now know it,

is not reality;
    earth is simply a dreamed-up world
where **angels** earn their wings.

Meanwhile, somewhere "back home,"
    you're snug as a bug, **peacefully** sleeping
        in the palm of God's hand,
surrounded by ancient friends who can't wait for
    you to **awaken** and tell the stories
        of who and where
  you thought you were.

And once everyone has had their turn,
    you'll all look at each other mischievously,
and whisper at the same time . . .

  "Let's . . . go . . . back!"

4

imagination,
dreams,
and baby steps

Every night for countless weeks over the summer before writing this book, we fought the same battle, with varying twists. You were Moana, from our favorite Disney film. In the shallow end of our swimming pool was your invisible family; they all loved and accepted me. I was Maui (also from *Moana*). Together, we'd cross turbulent seas toward my family, on the thick blue floatie, to the deep end where the bench was built into the side of the pool, trying to elude the murderous Kakamora pirates. Shortly into our quest, the volcano mistress Te Kā (she and the pirates were also of *Moana* and invisible) would rear her head, throwing massive molten lava rocks at us as we navigated to the far edge of the pool for safety. You'd scream. I'd scream. We'd fight back with all our might as the film's soundtrack blasted from patio speakers into the woods surrounding our home. Triumphant, you'd meet my family, who loved and accepted you, and we'd sail back to your family. Every night. For months.

What a production! What a summer! We were swept away by art imitating life imitating art. The magic of the ocean, so brilliantly portrayed by the writers of that great film, is exactly what I've been teaching adults, except that it works on land too. It exists for us, you're supposed to use it, it's intelligent, a friend, and it yearns to help you *help yourself*.

Implied repeatedly throughout the story was the fact that "the magic" could only help Moana when:

1. she had a dream—a specific vision, need, or goal,

2. she *really* cared, *emotionally*, about it (because she or her dream would otherwise *die*), and

3. she *first*, however feebly, took action.

Time and again she would physically throw herself into the ocean intending to save her island, or find

Maui, or retrieve the emerald heart of Te Fiti. A seemingly outrageous notion that this tiny, fragile person, flung into an ocean as wide as the planet, might make a difference. Yet because she did act, demonstrating belief and expectation, *the ocean responded.* Came alive. And exponentially magnified her efforts.

This is life's greatest manifesting secret, after passionately having a dream and caring about it, *you must act on it, even when you don't know what to do.* Even when it seems hopeless. Even when you don't know how your mortal "baby steps" could possibly make a difference.

Having a goal is easy. Caring about it is usually easy too. But taking action when it feels like your chances of success are infinitesimal—that takes a superhero. Only when you act does life's magic respond. You've got to have skin in the game, or there's no game. Do something, literally anything in the vague direction of your dream, *regularly and consistently,* and then, seemingly from nowhere, when you least expect, the magical winds of change begin to howl.

When the pool got too cold to swim in, your imagination would soar indoors. Some nights at bath time you were a rainbow kitty, colors revealed as if by magic once you were in the water. Other evenings we'd grab the kiddie paint and transform the aluminum ladder in the garage into an ever more beautiful pink, flowered staircase. To where? I didn't ask, because really, once you have a pink, flowered staircase, does it matter where it leads?

These were your stories, I was just the lucky guy who landed a co-starring role in the productions. And as I marvel now at our Academy Award–worthy performances, I'm rather amazed to realize that probably 97 percent of our adventures took place in our minds. I'm further wowed thinking that this ratio never changes throughout our life, no matter our age, no matter what we do.

What we want, what we fear, what we dream of, how we prepare, how we react, what we endure, what we decide, is almost *all* mental. Even if you're physically engaged in rigorous performances all day, every day, the mental planning, preparation, and evolving drama is still at least 97 percent of your experience ... by my admittedly not-remotely-scientific-certainly-underestimated measure. Right?

So, here's my offer. With life's *inner game* mastered early on, the rest of your life, the tiny part that shows up in time and space, will be a crazy-easy downhill slide. Perfecting your imagination to dream, to engage, to pretend, and to act. Sparking passion to inspire and ramp up a heightened sense of anticipation. Ultimately cultivating enough confidence that you believe in yourself and your journey, enabling resilience and patience, creating every opportunity for life's magic to reach and transform you.

Imagination *is* life. And yours will serve you well as you grow up—*especially when you know what you're doing.* Which is sure to happen if you stay true to yourself and you learn to tune out the voices that would strip you of believing in magic, make-believe, and the power of pretending. Keep your invisible friends. Be unpredictable. A tad unreasonable. Spontaneous. A dreamer.

Pay no attention to those who say life is hard. That we're here to be tested. That success is about survival of the fittest, hard work, and lucky breaks. That opportunity only knocks once. The early bird gets the worm. No matter how much those who say these things care about you.

Fortunately, the truth is a hard thing to lose. People, with all that they fear and all the limits they believe in, are still "irrationally" full of optimism. Fables and folklore insist that dreams come true, science now tells us that there's an energy to positive thinking, athletes are encouraged to visualize, in *The Secret* we talked about it as a universal law of attraction, and I've been telling people for 20 years that our thoughts *literally* become the things and events of our lives.

To repeat one of the most important lessons in this book, "thinking" is where and how you fit into the equation of reality creation. Learning how to "aim that thing" and calculating engagement is what this chapter is about. It's an add-on to chapter 2, with more specificity about the subtle art of breathing life into your dreams.

Imagine . . .

Time and space is where we chase things
    we **pretend** we don't have—
love, friends, and abundance—
    while worrying about things we pretend we do
    have—
problems, challenges, and issues.
    Until one day we **happen** to notice
the prophetic powers of pretending.

To **build** a mansion in time and space,
    whether of mortar, gold, or friendships,
think of imagination as your blueprint,
    desire as your **funding**,
faith as your builder, and action
    as proof these dots are being connected.

Treating any old job as if it were your dream job
    is the fastest way to spark the kind of life changes
that will yield your dream job.

Same for any old house, friend, day, life,
    or pair of espadrilles.

Great big, ear-to-ear, open-mouth smiles
    are responsible for far more sizzling romances,
        salary increases, life extensions
           and calorie burning
than our dentists, doctors, and financial planners
    will ever comprehend.

Smiling or laughing for no reason at all
    is one of the best reasons to smile or laugh—
plus, doing either will summon circumstances
    that will give you reason after reason.

Bringing new things into your life boils down to
learning to think of **yourself** with them.
And vice versa for removing things from your life.

Always speak of the past gratefully.
Of the future, excitedly.
And of the present, with **bobbing** eyebrows
and a Cheshire grin.

If anyone should ever ask if you're enlightened . . .
always say, "Yes!"
Same if they ask whether or not you're healthy,
wealthy, and loved **beyond** imagination.

When in **doubt**, show up early, think less, feel more,
ask once, give thanks, **expect** the best,
appreciate everything, never give up, make it fun, lead,
invent, regroup, wink, chill, smile,
and live as if your success were **inevitable,**
and so it shall be.

Creative visualization, as an exercise,
gives the biggest bang for the least effort.
Visualize, every weekday (you can take weekends off),
no **longer** than a few minutes,
imagine your dreamed-of end results,
as if they'd already come to pass,
fueled by emotion,
yourself in the picture,
smiling **broadly,**
happy tears running down your face.

If you're at **least** visualizing or meditating enough
  to wonder whether or not you're doing it right,
you're **doing** it right
  and you're way **ahead** of the game.

Every fortune, comeback, or kiss
  was first a thought, a **whisper,** a dream.
The trick with imagination is remembering to use it.

The secret to **living** the life of your dreams is
  to start living them at once, however humbly,
    to any **degree** you can.
If you can't travel far, travel near.
  If you can't dine out, go for dessert.
If you don't have a travel partner, be your **own.**

The secret to **performing** miracles lies in:
    1. Knowing your desired outcome.
        2. *Not* knowing how you'll pull it off.
           3. **Proceeding** anyway.

Should you ever be in need of a miracle,
    think not of the miracle, not even a little,
but instead of its intended **result**.

Little ducks never line up until momma duck just goes—
    the same will be **true** of getting
        your ducks in a row.

Rarely are the first **steps** in a journey anything like the
final ones, either in direction, pace, or grace.
Which means that none of those **things** are even
half as **important** as the fact
that there are steps at all.

Usually, if you just start "dancing,"
the "music" will be added—as will the partners,
a giant disco ball,
and **whatever** else you need.
Because the resources you need
to complete a **journey**
are only added once you begin it.

The **odd** thing about inspiration is
that it usually comes **after**, not before,
a new journey is **started**.

When **just** starting out on a new journey,
  it's only natural to feel vulnerable.
After all it may seem that you have much to lose.
  The **truth,** however, is that never again
at any other point in the same journey
   will you have so much to gain.

Don't let the dazzling **heights** you aspire
  to scare you from getting started.
Few could climb Mount Everest tomorrow,
  though virtually all could **begin** preparing.

It's more **important** to start,
  than to start in the **right** direction.

There's **nothing** you've ever done
    that wasn't significantly done for you,
        once you got **started**.
Remember that next time you're overwhelmed
    at the outset of a new adventure.

Most **big** ideas don't seem like big ideas at first.
    So, be on the lookout for little ones that seem
kind of ho-hum, let-me-floss-first kind of **ideas**.

Until the **really** great stuff comes along,
    do the not-so-great stuff,
because for those who dream big, the not-so-great stuff
    always leads to the really **great** stuff.

Great **big** innovative, world-changing
    ideas are plentiful.
People who take tiny little baby steps **toward** them
      are rare.

It's okay to dream big and start small—
    you'll probably **have** to.

The **real** reason so many have trouble
    with taking baby steps
is because they think those steps are
      important for the distance covered.
Not realizing that each one
    triggers enormous leaps and bounds
      taken on their behalf in realms unseen.

Life's magic isn't a substitute for networking,
    socializing, preparing, or cold calling.
To the contrary, these are some
    of its **greatest** incubators.

Don't be **afraid** to do the obvious.
    Not all miracles hide in the unseen.
Some hang around, **waiting** for you to call,
    write, or show up.

It's better to have loved and lost,
    tried and failed, dreamed and missed,
        than to sit out your turn in fear.
Because the loss, the failure,
    and the miss are only temporary,
whereas the love, the **adventure,** and the dream
        will never stop paying dividends.

You simply can't lose something
        you're still capable of giving.
You can't fail if you haven't stopped **trying**.
        And you can't miss if you're still aiming.

The thing that **most** forget,
        while dreamily looking off into the horizon
                for the **ship** of their dreams,
is that such ships never sail in,
        but are **built** beneath our very feet.

Here's a **little** "Inevitability Test" to check on the
        progress you're making toward achieving
                any particular dream:

You're pretty much **doing** something about it
        every single day.

Consistent **effort,** no matter how small,
sparks magic, fills sails,
butters bread, turns tides,
instills faith, summons friends, improves health,
burns calories, creates abundance, yields clarity,
builds courage, spins planets,
and rewrites **destinies.**

Opportunity never stops knocking.
And neither should you.

There are **more** than enough worms
for every bird, **early** and late.
What matters is that you keep **showing** up.

Thinking **big** but acting small
    is the same as thinking **small.**

It's not the size of your dreams that determines
    whether they come true,
but the size of the **actions** you take
    that imply their inevitable arrival.

Sometimes the hard way is really the easy way
    and the slow way is really the fast way.
Yet such sublime surprises may remain
    forever **unknown** if you just wait for the
quick and easy way.

Practice. Study. Prepare yourself.

Think. Act. Face your beasts.

Pay the piper whatever dues you think you have to pay.

Do the **dance,** walk the fire, wait in line.

Plant the seeds, hoe the field, go to market.

Because on the day that you become

all that you may ever **dream** of becoming,

there's simply no price you'd find too great.

The **anticipated** happiness

that moves you in the direction

of a new dream will **always** pale in comparison

to the actual happiness you'll find

once it comes **true.**

Which is **worth** trying to imagine, anyway.

The more you **push** yourself into areas of discomfort—
gently, just a bit, from time to time—
the more "comfortable" you'll become in those areas.

The **opposite** is also true.

Do not abandon the **tools** of intellect,
logic, and common sense,
but combine them with your feelings,
faith, and imagination.

Avoiding something draws it ever near.
Defending yourself can become a full-time job.
And worrying about things that **might** never happen
increases their chances of happening.

Never forget that all you may ever dream of having
is far less than what you **already** have.

Manifesting deadlines are fine
    when **placed** upon yourself,
like "write a new chapter every month,"
    as guides or goals,
but don't give **deadlines**
    to the Universe and its magic,
       like, "Have a publisher by year-end."
You simply cannot see enough of your dream's
    required logistics, in relation to
       all of your other desires,
and in relation to those of the world,
    to do so **effectively** without risking
       limitation or sacrificing other dreams.

The **greatest** trick and most subtle secret
    to doing anything really, **really** well
       is loving that you get to do it at all.

Do it **your** way, that's why you're here.

The **presumption**, at all times
      and under all circumstances, should always be that
you are good enough, worthy enough,
      and lovable enough.
And that you are exactly
      the **right** kind of person,
            in the right place, at the right time
                  to have the life you want.
Otherwise, you wouldn't have been given
            such dreams to begin with.

Sometimes **you'll** learn much more about life,
      love, and happiness,
- when you're single
      than when you're in a relationship,
- when you're **looking** for work
      than when you're working, and

- when you're confused
    rather than when you're clear . . .
. . . which doesn't mean don't seek change
    if you want there to be **change.**
It means, if you can allow yourself to learn what
    there is to **learn,** from wherever you now are,
        rather than resist,
you'll greatly accelerate
    your **dreamed** of transformation.

When you don't know what to do next,
    it might be because you've **already** done
more than you **give** yourself credit for,
    and it's time to chill out a bit.

Very **often** when you just can't decide between two
    or more options,
the answer that would give you the most peace
    . . . hasn't **yet** arrived.

Ask,

    yet expect.

Surrender,

    yet prepare.

       And **miracles** will abound.

The **only** way to get what you really want

    is to know what you really want.

And the only way to know what you really want

    is to **know yourself.**

And the only way to know yourself is to be yourself.

    And the only way to be yourself is to

       listen to your **heart.**

Enjoying short-term pleasures
    to the detriment of long-term dreams
is as crazy as pursuing long-term dreams
    to the detriment of short-term pleasures.
Both are important.

Impatience is a sign
    that you've temporarily forgotten
to behave at all times as if your dreams
        have already come true.

The more you hurry, the slower you go.
    The more you wait, the longer it takes.

It's **totally** possible to have big,
    huge, gigantic dreams,
yet still be deliriously **happy**
    before they come true.

Sometimes, when things take longer
    than you thought they would,
it's just a reminder from your **higher** self that you
    have more time than you thought and that
there's a journey to enjoy.

The **shortest** distance between here and there—
    or between today and the life of your wildest
    dreams—runs through **joy.** Be led by it.

When you **hang** out in time and space long enough,
     you'll inevitably learn it's through the twin gateways of
          persistence and **patience**
               that masters become masters.

Persistence is priceless,
     but its value lies in doing, doing, **doing**,
          not in waiting, waiting, waiting.
Not knocking on one door until it opens,
     but knocking on **all** of them
          until one opens.

Whenever **spending** or investing,
   whether a little or a lot, wisely or not,
remember to celebrate that you're
   creating **opportunities,**
      exchanging energy, dancing with life
supporting economies, feeding families,
   lessening poverty, demonstrating courage,
validating others, eradicating fear, inviting magic,
   and lifting humanity higher into the **light.**

Actually, **creating** wealth is even
   more fun than spending it,
so be sure to daydream as much about the former
   as the **latter.**

The best way to **manifest** money,
   which is just as true for manifesting love,
is to focus less on these by-products of
   a life well lived and more on a
      life well **lived.**

It's not **thinking** about the bucks
    that makes one rich,
but thinking rich that **makes** the bucks.

It takes a really **special** person to find true happiness
    in the lap of luxury, surrounded by friends
        and laughter, and choices, choices, choices.
And oddly, it's **usually** the exact same kind of person
    who could have been equally happy without all that,
spending time alone, **maybe** with a book,
    or some tools, or a dog.

The **self-made** millionaire invariably
    thinks about income **more** than expenses.
And probably about customers, more than vendors;
    possibilities more than risks;
smiles more than frowns;
    options more than commitments;
vacations more than overtime;
    detours more than setbacks;
        opportunities more than obstacles.

It's **okay** to love material things;
　　matter is pure spirit, only more so,
because you've thought about it so much,
　　you've **brought** it to "life."

The most **surefire** way to find yourself,
　　make a **friend**,
　　　　turn a buck,
　　　　　　and discover your **power**
is to help someone else do the same.

One of the most advanced forms of self-help
　　is **helping** others.
So please, when in doubt or when in trouble,
　　"help **yourself.**"

True selfishness is
    honoring God's
        unique expression in you,
which will ensure that as the winds of divinity
    are blown through your **heart,**
the **melody**
    is unlike any other.

To **care** for self *at the expense* of others
    is not selfishness, but ignorance.
We all depend to some degree
    upon the **whole**
        to truly prosper,
and when any one of us suffers,
    all suffer.

Living deliberately starts with imagining your
dreams
as if they have already come **true.**
It's a matter of switching gears, never looking back,
and *being* the person that you've always dreamed
you'd be.
Predicating your behavior on *their* reality,
not the old illusions that will still surround you.

Living your life from *their* mind-set.
Entertaining every thought,
saying every word,
and making every decision from *their* point of view.
Walking the way they would **walk,**
dressing the way they would dress,
and spending your **free** time
the way they would spend theirs.

Frequently, in time and space,
  right before a really HUGE dream comes true
    . . . nothing seems to be happening.

So if, perchance, it ever appears as if
  absolutely nothing is happening in your life,
particularly after you've been dreaming big
  and taking action . . .
    consider it . . .

    a sign.

Probably the most important thing I could tell you
  about living the life of your dreams,
would be to point out that
  you already are.

5

making the
most
of friends, family
& relationships

You won't remember this, you were two. We were at the kids' park playing follow the leader, each of us jostling to be at the front of our two-person conga line, when a little boy about your size walked into our space, causing us to stop while you stared at him, then at me, then at him, before asking in a hopeful tone without malice, "Daddy, can you make him disappear?"

And then there was the time, at the same park a few months later, when you timidly drifted from me toward the two slightly older girls sitting and chattering away in the sand-filled, vacated volleyball court with dolls and shovels. I watched as you approached, eyebrows raised, in your first self-chosen social encounter of your own creation, about to connect with new best friends formulating the most magical words you could imagine to greet them, probably, "My name is Rebecca. That's my daddy," as was your go-to self-identifying phrase around strangers . . . when suddenly, as if these two you approached were cleverly disguised samurai sword–carrying ninja warriors, with the spin of her head toward you, the leader cleaved you in half, pronouncing you unworthy: *"No. Not here. GO!"* Shredding your heart and mine with her unceremonious words. Her execution was so abrupt, I fleetingly hoped you didn't understand, except the command was punctuated with a snap of her extended arm and pointed finger telling you exactly which way to depart.

Frozen in shock and grief, your fragile smile replaced by a grimaced awkwardness, unable to step in any direction, the building anguish so great you couldn't speak your name or even cry to me, tears welling as you tried to maintain your composure, I saw you die in defeat. Until you did cry, uncontrollably, withering into my fast-approaching arms. Your pain was deep. Heartbroken. Confused. Sad. Suffering. Devastated. And utterly inconsolable.

I tried to tell you it didn't matter, that they were not being nice, that they were unworthy of your interest, that there were other, more fun things for us to do. That life was still beautiful, the sun was still shining, the day was not done . . . but you couldn't hear me. I frantically wondered what else I could do to minimize the crippling memory and lasting scar of this fateful day . . .

Fifteen minutes later you were fine. *What?*

I wonder, though, if you'll have the same recovery time when you're 15? 25? Older? With *understanding*, of both self and life, it could be the same—if you'd even allow yourself to feel so hurt by the fickle behavior of others in the first place. Because with understanding you'd know to rely on yourself for approval. You'd find that what others say and do reflects their issues, not yours. And you'd learn that you are more than what happens on any step of your life's path; you are more, even, than the path itself. With understanding you'll better be able to see yourself *as I now see you,* which will remind you always of how deeply you're loved.

✿ Little will add to your life as much as your relationships, although what you gain, when, how, and with who, won't always be as predictable as you'd like, nor will your gains necessarily coincide with what you hoped to be receiving. And little else will build you up as much or tear you down as quickly as what you learn from love. Until, in the end, with a heart that learns to be open and vulnerable, you'll find that it was you, all along, who did the building and tearing.

Not that others won't have a role, given by you, to assist in your "construction." And conversely, you'll often be granted roles in helping to shape the lives of others. Understand, however, that no one can come into our lives who's not preapproved. Their probable actions and behaviors known in advance of whenever your paths may cross.

Which is to say, that while you're the ultimate authority of what happens in your life, one of your more clever levers for effecting this, will be who you draw or allow into your adventure, and what behaviors you help to elicit from them through your own thoughts, words, and deeds.

Sounds complicated, but it's not. All you need to take from this, is that those in your life are "on board" with your manifestations and lessons, present and future, just as you are for theirs. True teammates. Love bound, however you may fumble or offend. Your needs, fears, and passions are intertwined. Compatible. Complementary. Today. Tomorrow . . . minds may change.

In this chapter I'll share what I've learned in my life on love, rejection, longing, sharing, disappointment, compromise, commitment, and moving on. But no matter how much I may open your heart to the little I know about love, you will still, for the rest of your life, persistently desire to have certain people appear in, or disappear from, yours, and to have them otherwise behave in certain preferable ways. They will have similar wishes of you.

Throughout, remember who you really are to each other. Kindred spirits drawn together in the romantic adventure of life. Fellow actors lost in these illusions to learn what's true and real. Honor each other. Enjoy the camaraderie. Treat one another with the same kindness and respect you hope to be afforded. Understand that just as others might hurt you out of confusion, so will you them. And as much as you'd like to hear apologies or to be forgiven, so would they.

In the meantime, no matter who else comes or goes from your adventure, please know I'll *always* be there, in one form or another, to catch you when you fall, send angels when you call, and love you through it all.

You're simply the greatest.

you are loved

If **everyone** really knew
    how much they were **loved,**
        not only from "**above,**"
            but by those now in their life,
there'd be **little** hearts drawn on everything
    from wheelbarrows to skyscrapers to jumbo jets.

When something **hurts** your eyes,
    stop looking at it.
When it hurts your ears, **stop** listening to it.
    And when it hurts your heart,
        stop **justifying** it.

In the **beginning,** the price of giving great love
    is risking that it won't be returned.
In the end, however, you'll find great love
    is always **returned.**

To **err** on the side of generosity, patience,
    love, or **kindness** is not to err.

If you could **actually** stand in someone else's shoes
    to hear what they hear, see what they see,
and feel what they feel, you would **honestly** won-
    der what **planet** they live on
and be blown away by how different their
    "**reality**" is from yours.

You'd also never, in a million years, be quick to
    judge again.

Being happy without a partner
is the fastest way to attract one.
If you even want one.

One of **love's** many corollaries is that the brighter
your light, the more you attract
... **everything.**
Moths and butterflies.
At which **point** you begin learning what to celebrate
and what to let **fly** on by.

There is no such thing as an **ideal**
relationship status,
except yours, today, for now.

Of **all** the reasons you might draw someone into
your life, one would never be to
find their faults.

Putting up your defenses will inspire others
to put up their **offenses.**

Sometimes it may **help** to see difficult people
as reminders of what you may have
put **others** through.
Or to see grouchy people as those who may have
chosen a more challenging life than you.

When you look for what's **right**—in others,
in relationships, in yourself, and in your journey—
you'll always **find** it.

Same when you look for what's **wrong.**

You may not ever understand what's going
on in "their" life,
but you can always figure out what's going on in yours.
Let their shortcomings inspire you
to work on your own.

Sometimes, the person whose life looks the easiest
has had it the hardest,
but they're really good at not dwelling on the past,
living in the moment,
having dreams for tomorrow,
and "rolling like that."

Always, the **strong** carry the weak,
    the rich carry the poor,
        the healthy carry the sick,
and the happy carry the sad.

And it's probably because this was once
    their **promise**,
to **thank** those who earlier carried them.

Everyone gets carried a little bit, which is some-
    thing to remember when it's your turn to carry.

Seeing things from someone else's **perspective**
    can totally **change** your life.
Which might even explain why they're in yours
    to begin with.

In your **times** with others you'll laugh and cry,
    and in your times alone you'll understand why—
let there be **both.**

Arguments are won intellectually, **not** love.

Being fair and reasonable
    will earn you respect and admiration,
but being genuinely **kind**
    will make you a total love **magnet.**

Ask with love
      and their answer may surprise you.

Hear with **love**
      and your answer may surprise them.

Simply **dwelling** upon joy, abundance,
      or anything else that might involve other people
will literally draw complete strangers into your life
      who will **bring** those things,
   when in alignment with all else you **dwell** upon.

At all times and in all places, be the **first** to smile.

While it's often **fashionable**
    to dwell upon what might have been,
what's usually not **understood** is that,
    really and truly, it couldn't have.

Most of the time when people think the present
    could have been **different** than it is,
it's because they think the past was different than it was.

Be **glad** things went as they did—
    you still have forever.

When someone **treats** you differently
    than you expected,
it's usually because you've **been**
    sending out **mixed** signals.

No matter what you do that may disappoint
    or hurt others,
always keep in mind, it was the very best you could
    have done, with what you **knew** at the time.

And so will this be **true** of others
    who disappoint or hurt **you.**

When it comes to **choosing** who will be in your life,
    be sure to value their "Cowabunga!"
quality as much as all others.

The more it seems "love hurts,"
    the more you can be sure it's something else,
like pride, fear, or not remembering
    how **fabulous** you are.

Those in **great** relationships aren't always those
who are good at relationships.
And those in **challenging** relationships
aren't always those who are bad at relationships.

No matter how great the **desire** is to please another,
let it be no greater than the desire to **be** yourself.

Don't **trust** anyone who tells you your happiness is
more important to them than their **own.**

When you **finally** see what this whole
    time-space thing is all about,
you're going to laugh; you're going to cry;
    and you're going to be so very **grateful**
you LOVED as much as you did.

There's nothing **unspiritual**
    about ending a relationship, for any reason
        or for no reason,
so long as you do it with **love**.

No one **owes** anyone anything.
> No matter who they are.
>> No matter what they've done.

No matter how **much** they may claim
> to suffer without you.

Those who **deserve** your love the least
> are usually the ones who need it the **most**.

Some, however, are better loved at a **distance**.
> For a while, anyway.

Fortunately, **love** doesn't really know the difference.

The **lower** the price of your love, the higher its value;
> the fewer the conditions, the **greater** its reach.

The criteria for **unleashing** torrents
   of love upon thine enemy
lies first in knowing that there should be no **criteria.**

When love is otherwise hard to feel for someone,
   allow it to **begin** with sympathy.

Your "**soul mate**" might not be the same person
   throughout your life,
and sometimes it **might** just be you.

Only do those things you **want** to do,
   with **whom** you want to do them.

Always **follow** your heart,
    unless it's been **broken.**
Then you must lead it.
    Back into love.

Hearts are never too big to mend,
    too small to rebound,
or too tired to love **again.**

When the **choice** is to hurt or be hurt,
    cheat or be cheated, violate or be violated,
always, always, **always** choose the latter.
    And then try to figure out how you created such
a fork in the road of your **life** to begin with.

Always, kindness prevails—
    no matter how things **appear,**
nor how humbling a task,
    nor how **unkind** they've been.

When someone **speaks**
    on a topic unfamiliar to you,
you might be able to gauge the **honesty** and accuracy
    of their words by all else they've ever shared
with **you** on topics you were familiar with.

Same **for** authors.

Sometimes, **expecting** a straight answer from
    some people is absolutely out of the question.
Which should answer your **question.**

It's **always** best to assume that everyone either
knows the truth, or will know the **truth,**
because they either do or they will.

When you **understand** that your disappointment
    in another's behavior always stems from
their immaturity, or **yours,**
    rather than their unkindness, or yours,
it becomes much harder not to keep **skipping**
    through life, giddy with joy, smelling the flowers.

When someone **behaves** poorly, it's always because
    they've forgotten how **powerful** they really are,
how **beautiful** life is, or how much they're loved.

The best way to **deal** with other people . . .
is to just let them be **other** people.

The **only** person who should ever have to live by
your standards, is **you**.
Let everyone else off the hook.

At this **very** moment
there are people only you can reach.
Some of whom may have chosen this very **lifetime**
hoping you'd be in theirs.

One of the most **helpful** things you can do
for another is to let them
learn their lessons for **themselves,**
at their own pace.
It's **also** one of the most helpful things
you can do for **yourself.**

The most **effective** way of changing another
person, though not guaranteed,
comes from changing how **you** see them.

If you **don't** really *have to* change someone
to keep on loving them, then don't.
Because trying to **change** one thing about them
might change **other** things about them.

For as long as you **wish** to
    keep someone in your life,
       whoever they may be,
understanding them,
    as opposed to changing them,
       will wildly improve **chances**
they'll wish to keep you in their life.

How you treat **people,** in general,
    is the single biggest factor for determining
how people, in general, will **treat** you.

This does not always work, however,
    in **one-on-one** relationships.

Expecting and *preparing*
  for someone's very best behavior—
    in **terms** of respect, kindness, love,
or just winning their attention
        —guarantees nothing.
But wildly improves your chance of
    receiving it . . .

. . . better, if you don't **insist** that such behavior
  come from a specific **person,**
chances of receiving it from someone else
      "as good or better,"
        at the right time,
          are 100 **percent.**

✼

Nothing you might ever do
  can ensure anyone **else's** happiness.

✼

It's **not** that people will act a **certain** way around you,
    but that you'll attract certain **types** of people and
behaviors based upon your thoughts, beliefs,
    and **expectations** of them.

When you **change,**
    the people you attract and their behaviors
        will change.

A **kind** word can move mountains
    and change lives.
But for those times when they **escape** you,
    when the right thing isn't said,
        or the time wasn't right to say it,
kind **thoughts** can do the same.

Thoughts have a way of lingering,
    seeking, and **finding**
        their intended beneficiary,
unfettered by time and space.

Your **kind** thoughts and deeds toward others—
    like sharing a smile, a compliment,
        or a helping hand—
plant seeds of beauty, **hope,** and love
    that will one day grow into a spectacular garden
      that *you* will get to call **home.**

Forgiveness is **only** necessary when first there's blame.
    And blame can only be **cast**
      when first there's misunderstanding.

Better to accept that at some level,
    for some reason, you chose to participate
in whatever happened between you and someone else,
    and thereby reclaim your **power,**
than to abdicate responsibility through a false belief
    that bad things can happen to good people,
      setting yourself up for another fall.

As is true of **kissing,**
    let your life know both spontaneity
        and thoughtfulness.

Sexual orientation is like being
    left- or right-handed—
it's not random, it will **serve** you,
    and you are far, far **more** than any orientation.

Good looks have less to do with one's body
    and more to do with one's **mind.**

Looks **change,** beauty **lasts.**

Sometimes, more can be **learned**
    from the disagreeable than the agreeable.

Any profound **difference** you make
    in the life of someone else
        will always be **smaller** than
the difference it will **make** in your own.

Success is better measured in **smiles** received,
giggles heard, and hands held
than in dollars earned, deadlines met,
and weight **lost**.

Know everyone by their good traits.

Sometimes, it's not just **about** finding the perfect
friend, partner, or tribe,
but finding the **perfection**
in **those** you've already found.

See everyone you meet as a brand-new chance
    to **fall** in love
        for a different **reason** than ever before.

❦

Friends are friends because they've discovered
    how much they have in **common.**
Enemies are friends too,
    who've not yet **discovered** this.

❦

For **anyone**, ever, to be in your life,
    you have something to **gain.**
        Besides their absence.

Although your **acquiring** the self-confidence to say,
"I love you, good-bye," might be a reason.

If you can see the little girl or little boy in another,
you'll probably **find** that the mask they wear
isn't to inspire your fear, but to **hide** their own.

Sometimes, **understanding** their fears,
helps you to understand
their pain and their behavior.
And understanding their **fears** sometimes helps
you to understand your own.

The next time someone upsets you, think to yourself,
Thanks for pointing out that I've begun depending on you.

And the next time someone doesn't take your view into account, think,
That's okay, I was once like that.

And if someone steals from you, think,
It was nothing, my supply is the Universe . .

. . . or lies to you, think,
I'm sorry you feel that need.

Violates you,
All for my growth and glory.

Is rude to you,
Cheer up, dear soul, it'll be okay.

Judges you,
Thanks for sharing.

Drives by you like a bat out of hell,
Be careful, my friend, you are loved.

And the next time someone greets you with a smile, smile back, like you're sharing a great secret.

The great thing about feeling **deep,**
    earthshaking love . . .
        is that you can start with anyone.

Send them **love.**
    Wish them peace. See them **happy.**

Everyone, always, forever.

6

what
old souls
know

Dream.

I'm not an "old soul," but you might be. It's an expression, of course, that universally means a kinder person, typically more patient, thoughtful and wise than most, presumably from lots of earthly experience. Perhaps, some speculate, experience that spans many lifetimes.

It's harder to know the soul age of kids because you were all so recently on the other side, "closer" to Source, from which we all emerged. Your worldview is less complicated than grown-ups'. I remember my niece, Sarah, when your age—upon learning of death and giving it some thought—suddenly blurted out, "Mommy, I know what happens when we die!"

"What, honey? What happens when we die?"

"We go back to normal!"

We're a *long way* from normal right now. But imagine, as I've already shared, it was from "normal" that we chose to come here. In our existence prior to entering the illusions, as the God-particles we had to have been, in pure radiance and light. Even from here we can deduce that back then we had to have been pretty amazing, in all of our glory, everywhere, always, at once, with thoughts that spontaneously changed everything, showered in love and knowing it, metaphorically in the palm of God's hand. *Pure* God, ourselves. There's only one thing that could rival that, make it better, even, exploding all possibilities into even more possibilities . . . *voluntarily losing ourselves to be here.* On one condition, of course: Our return to "normal" must be guaranteed. Otherwise, who would ever leave?

My little brain cannot conceive of anything, in all creation, not in any sphere of existence, that might be as audacious and brilliant as being born into time and space without any recollection of our divinity.

Having to find our own way when lost, our own courage when frightened, and the infinite powers at our disposal when challenged. Left to the elements to rediscover our supremacy over them. Driven by our passions so that we might rise above our humble, naked beginnings and ultimately see through the illusions that have hypnotized us. Only to find ourselves once again high upon the throne of "thy kingdom come" (used to be a Catholic, loved the pageantry), from whence it all began.

The deepest truth, of course, is that we never left our throne or stopped being pure God. *Not remembering this*, however, is the kicker that has made our adventures possible.

I want you to start remembering.

You have your work cut out for you. To give some context to the times you've landed in: taken as a whole, I'd say the soul age of the world today is still quite young, comparable to an individual in his or her late teenage years learning about responsibility and consequence. Easy to judge by simply observing our collective behavior.

Obviously, we're in a precarious orbit. At a critical point in shaping our destiny, which hinges entirely on the private and collective decisions we make that increasingly have global implications. Of course, we knew what we were getting into, born when we were, that the world would be moving from darkness into the light, from confusion and fear into truth and love; that we'd be alive at the dawn of our species' spiritual awakening. And you, born when you were, knew, given our natural propensity to self-correct and thrive, there'd still be a great likelihood of stunning advances in every field of humanity during this very lifetime.

Knowing this will hopefully ground and reassure you. What matters most, however, are *your* choices in this lifetime, not who you were and what you did in others. Facing today's fears. Living today's dreams. Creating new stories. Understanding yourself. The lessons that follow in this chapter are meant to move you to those ends, as I aim to whittle down the list of questions you might still have.

These observations and conclusions were arrived at in the same way as the earlier chapters, through blending experience, logic, and intuition. I've found throughout my life that by holding on to questions long enough, particularly ones that doubled me over in angst or awe, the answers I sought inevitably arrived. Here, again, my ideas are not unique; you'd arrive at them on your own should you have the interest, yet to offer you a boost so that you might peer from "my shoulders," perhaps even into realms I cannot yet see, I humbly continue.

Good God almighty!

In all **battles** between the heart and mind,
    go with your **heart.**
For truly, it's a lot easier for your mind
    to catch up with your heart,
than for your heart to catch up with your **mind.**

Step one for **changing** the entire world is
    falling in love with it as it **already** is.

Same for changing yourself.

Sometimes a **lack** of clarity,
    is actually the clarity you were in **need** of.

The **older** the soul, the softer the glance,
　　the quicker the **smile**, and the sooner to **say**,
　　　　"I love you."

They also tend to hold hands
　　with those they walk beside.

When **pondering** the vastness of the cosmos,
　　keep in mind that it goes even farther **inward**
than outward.

You can **usually** tell an old soul
　　by how indifferent they are to setbacks
and by how **friendly** they are to trees.

Young souls use pain to learn how things are.
　　Mature souls use pain to learn

how **else** things might be.
And **old** souls use pain to learn
how else they might be.

Random **awkwardness**, unexpected shyness,
feared inadequacy, and occasional blushing
are just a few **signs** that a
giant is settling into their **greatness.**

Always **listen** to your doubts.
Not just because they might **teach** you of your fears
but because, sometimes, they might teach you
of your **wisdom.**

Those who say, "I don't know what to do,"
usually do **know** what to do.

Disappointment **without** anger
is the mark of an old soul.

Not being disappointed
is the mark of a really old soul.

And **trusting** life so thoroughly
that every step on its path is valued
more than where it was supposed to take you,
is the mark of eternal youth.

Of all the things that really and **truly** matter,
working efficiently and getting more done
is **not** among them.

The **day** will come, if it hasn't already,
 when nothing else will matter to you as much
as helping others to succeed and
 to find the **happiness**
 you have found.

You only have to **ride** the wave of life,
 not **create** it.

Nine out of ten old souls **agree** that one of
 the very best things about spiritual maturity
is appreciating that age is so very meaningless.

The tenth soul?
 Out **climbing** trees and couldn't be reached.

The best way to **create** more free time,
    is to **take** it.

To move a **mountain,**
    befriend it, him, or her.

Everything that's ever **happened** to you,
    up until reading these very words, was just practice
for the really **good** stuff that's to follow.

Each **blossom** still blooms in its field,
each child still clutches your hand,
and each friend still lingers in your **heart**.

Just because a window of **time** has closed
doesn't mean what it showed you is gone.

You needn't be **intimidated** by your dreams
or scared by your fears,
because in a world of illusion,
where you are **their** creator,
you are also their **greater**.

When **driving** down the road of life,
rarely do you know how **good** you have it,
until you see it in the rearview mirror.
Unless you **remember** this mid-drive,
which should be right about **now.**

Young **souls** look to secrets, rites, and rituals.
Mature souls look to science, math,
and **evidence.**
And old souls just look **within.**

The **pursuit** of money as a means to anything
    should always be secondary
to the pursuit of the thing **itself**.

The sun asks not that the moon and planets
    help **brighten** each day
but relishes her role as a **keeper** of the light
    and a bringer of the dawn.
A role, no doubt, that will be much like **your** own.

Some **people** bloom late. Some very late.
    And some, very, very late. But, they all **bloom**.
And the **longer** it takes, the more spectacular it is.

Dimming your **light** in sadness or empathy
over the suffering of others **doesn't** help anyone.

Sometimes it's your downtime,
lounging-in-bed-too-long time, walkabout time,
watching-the-rain time and blow-Friday-off time
that makes possible your **greatest** achievements.

When you **give** yourself permission
to be totally unproductive,
and you actually **relish** such interludes,
your genius, creativity, and productivity
will **increase** exponentially.

A sign that you're **approaching** enlightenment,
  beyond auras, ringing bells, and a healing touch,
is that you start valuing idle daydreaming
  as **much** as you value being
    in the throes of creativity.

And that you begin talking **sweetly,**
  not only to plants and trees,
    but to cars and toasters and computers.

You find you're **eagerly**
  picking up trash in public places.

And, **quite** unequivocally, you begin to feel grati-
  tude for present challenges,
    love for lousy drivers,
and sympathy for those who don't see
  service in their work.

Until you arrive, **then,** these might be ways to lean in.

It's **perfectly** okay, and sometimes highly ideal,
to claim all is well amid doubt and confusion.
To be happy in spite of challenges.
To **laugh** at problems.
Dance without a partner.
Sing without a rhyme.
And talk to inanimate **objects.**

You might be an old soul when,
in spite of the usual challenges,
you'd be **happy** to live another 10,000 lifetimes,
even though your learning is almost done.
Whereas feeling impatience or **boredom**
usually means you've got more living to do.

While you **may,** from time to time, envy others, it's
precisely during those moments when you
might ask yourself
whether or not you'd actually like to **be** them.
And your **envy** will be cured.

Gorgeous, **magnificent,** and *sublime* are words that
should be used as frequently as possible
between you and your mirror.

Hubba, hubba is good too.
And please never forget to **smile.**

For a **long** time yet, there will be things
    not to like in time and **space** . . .
animal testing, war, discrimination,
    hatred, to name a **few.**
But please **realize,** only while living
    can you do anything about them.

When it comes to **climbing** mountains,
    slaying dragons,
        or just plain getting what you want,
remember, you've got a built-in, double-secret
    advantage:

        You're supernatural.

In the **truest** sense,
　　　the world around you
　　　　　is **just** more you.

Just because all things are possible,
　　　doesn't mean you're supposed to do all **things**.
Besides, it's not like you **aren't** going to live forever.

Your **feelings** are your choice,
　　　what manifests thereafter may not be.
Choose wisely.

Young souls value people for their productivity,
mature souls value people for their wisdom,
and old souls value people.

Early societies live by the Rule of Might,
and the strong prevail.
Advanced societies live by the Rule of Law,
and the privileged prevail.
Enlightened societies live by the Rule of Love,
and everyone thrives.

Apologize to an old soul
and your gesture will be honored.
Apologize to a young soul
and matters may become even more complicated.
Apologize anyway.

What if every wrinkle, scar, and gray hair
   made you more beautiful?
Every tear shed, mistake made, and challenge faced
   drew you closer to the light?
And every breath taken, sentence spoken,
      and path chosen
sparked uproarious cheering from behind
         the curtains of time and space?

      They do.

Taking full responsibility for your life includes
   never forgetting to have fun.

The novice **learns** to be honest with others,
    in terms of who, what, when, and where.

The **advanced** soul learns to be honest with self,
and discovers that "perspective" rules,
    yet changes **swiftly**.
The **master,** however, studies honesty in terms of
motivation, where heretofore,
    the lies have really piled **up**.

It's **not** what's said that determines whether
    you're being honest, but **why** you said it.
For example, if someone told you it's a beautiful day,
    to distract your attention from the dent they just
put in your car door, they'd be lying.

Never make a **decision** until you have to.

People who give are given to.
   People who care are cared for.
And people who **love** . . .
   age slower, run faster, **jump** higher,
are as happy with friends as they are alone,
   climb more trees, **skip** when they could walk,
kiss when they could talk,
   take the odd Friday off,
experience faster **manifestations,**
   and are really popular with animals.

Being **worthy** isn't something you earn,
   it's something you **recognize.**

Always see work as play
and play as **important,**
and soon you won't know the difference between them.

A "forever being" would never worry about the future,
look back and regret,
or have anything, ever, to fear.
Unless they forgot they're **forever.**

Upon **hearing** criticism, the beginner scorns it.
The careful student **weighs** it.
And the master says, "But, of course!"
understanding she attracted it and therefore
needed to hear it, **whether** it was true or not.

Never has a **word** been uttered
    that didn't have meaning to the ears
        who **heard** it.

Offering criticism belies a **longing** for
    recognition, appreciation, and validation.
None of which, **however,** can be obtained
        through **criticism.**

Thinking that the death of a loved one
    is unfortunate, ill-timed,
        sad for the departed, or **random**
is to deny the perfection and **order**
    that are otherwise so abundantly
        obvious throughout these magical **jungles**
        of time and space.

From time to **time,** as your life allows,
   try not to be too practical, **logical,** or predictable.

Often, that **which** you misunderstand is drawn to you.
   Never because you "needed" the **lesson,**
nor because all must be so initiated,
   but because there had been **earlier** thoughts
      of awe, wonder, or criticism.
And such thoughts, as all thoughts must,
   will rearrange your life to bring you more
      of **whatever** you were thinking of.
And then, in attracting what you didn't understand,
   you will ultimately gain enough **clarity**
      to understand it, release it,
         and **finally,** be free of it.

Spirituality should not be sought to avoid
the material world, but to better **engage** it.

Sometimes the **people** who know,
don't know they know.
And sometimes the people who don't know, **think**
they do. But you can always tell who is which,
because with **knowing** comes kindness.

A test that **reveals** whether or not those in your
company are truly enlightened is whether or
not they **treat** others as if they,
too, are **truly** enlightened.

The **primary** roles of love are not to heal,
    fix, or mend.
Not to soothe, cure, or ease.
Not even to refresh, rejuvenate, or restore.
    The primary roles of love are to
        "Yahoo!" "Yee-haa!"
            and "Whoo-hoo!"

The **difference** between a young soul and an old soul
    is only known by the old **soul,**
        who would never breathe a word of it.

The most fun a baby soul can have
     comes from **having.**

The most fun a young soul can have
     comes from **doing.**

And the most fun an old soul can have
     comes from **being—**
          which usually leads to lots of having and doing.

Ultimate life **mastery** eventually becomes
     more a function of knowing **what** to want,
than knowing how to **get** what you want.

It's being **alive** that makes you rich.

If an event was so super-extraordinarily rare
    and **fantastically** incredible
    that it only happened once every 10 *billion* years,
it would still be infinitely more ordinary, routine,
    and credible than the **passage** of any given day.

An enlightened **soul** is not one
    to whom truth has been **revealed,**
but one who has summoned it.

A little heads-up on an affliction
    that **afflicts** all really old souls:
Giving love, eventually, becomes a much **greater**
    need than receiving it.

Whenever conferring with another—
    either face-to-face or across the miles—
whether a human being, departed spirit,
    or sentient tree,
        always speak to the **highest** within them.

(Right, as if some trees weren't sentient. Nice catch.)

When **you** distrust,
   you **attract** the untrustworthy.

The very first **inkling** you may have
   that you were actually born into
      "spiritual **royalty**"
comes when you notice there are flowers
   only you can pick.
   Butterflies only you can **see**.
Laughter and tears only you can know.
   And dreams only you can make **real**.

Let every season run its course
   and every tide ebb and flow,
      but think not that you have no choice
         of where your wandering mind may go.

In other words, letting life happen
   doesn't mean giving up your power.

The reason most people worry so much,
   is because there exists between them and life
a passionate love affair.

If ever **granted** one wish, wish for what is,
    because nothing will ever be **better** than living
in a world where the past doesn't matter,
    the future can be **anything**,
        and your thoughts become **things**.

The **trick** to being in the right place, at the right time,
    is knowing you **already** are.

It always works, there's **only** love,
    things are getting **better,** you chose well,
there've been **no** mistakes, you're never alone,
    and everything makes you **more**.

You can be quite sure,
      given the *infinite* choices available at the time
and your celestial connection with the Divine,
         that long ago, when you carefully mapped out
               your present adventure into the
                  jungles of time and space;
the hills and valleys you would likely traverse;
the setbacks and advances you would likely encounter;
      the good, the bad, and the ugly,
               and all of the lives you would touch;
when your planning was done
         and the "big picture" **revealed** . . .

. . . you **burst** into tears of **joy**,
overwhelmed by its perfection and who you'd become.

Savor the uncertainties.
 Seize the possibilities.
  Seek.
   Wander.
    Explore.
    Ask.

  Face your fears.

Don't rush love
 or force details.

Take risks.
  Be exceedingly kind.
   Move with your dreams.

You have what it takes to
 be whoever you feel called to be.
  Your full presence is needed;
   you were chosen to live amid these very days,
    as much as you chose.

You are inclined to succeed
 and your success will inspire others
  to do the same.

You are who God most wanted to be.
 And still does.

epilogue

the
man
i am

    Two years ago, at the local science center, we were both deep into the three-story-tall transparent human-hamster house, that really was for kids taller than you, and not for adults at all. As in earlier visits, your zeal for adventure had us both lost inside. Like usual, hunched over, cramming myself into the barrel hallways and spiral climbs, I was one of the few, if any, parents inside.

Especially endearing were your repeated calls for me to follow you whenever I slowed, your hand blindly reaching behind you to receive mine, "Daddy, Daddy, come on, Daddy!" There was no shame or embarrassment that I was with you. To the contrary, I was the cool enabler of your adventures—besides, you hadn't reached that age yet. Each time you called, the sound of your voice quickened my pace and filled my heart, helping me to forget the physical pain of the assignment.

About an hour into it—an *hour*—my knees and back and neck were so tired, I casually let the space between us increase and you silently "let me slide," aware but ignoring, or so I thought, the distance growing between us.

Before too long, I was on the outside, looking in. When possible, I watched and trailed under you, far above me, though you were no longer reachable. It was clear you were getting quite good at navigating this thing and didn't really need me. Similarly, while the first few times it was fun for me to go inside as the doting, appreciated father, I'd had my fill. From the viewpoint of comfort, yours as much as mine, we probably let our playing and mutual dependency go on longer than necessary. Yet we were both happy to have spent a little extra time together, ensuring attainment of this point between dependence and release. That you'd still call for me from time to time, as if to need me . . . sweet bliss.

Without any warning whatsoever, a trace thought in my mind rapidly grew into a man-eating beast, and suddenly, I was gutted. It happened as you climbed alone up a level, from the second to the third, and began to leverage yourself around an obstacle, not that there was any connection between what you were doing and what I was thinking. It dawned on me that this process leading to independence is exactly what it'll be like once you grow up, ready to leave our home. That the father-daughter relationship is a functional one. A job, fulfilling, joyful—especially joyful—to share life with you, to guide and help you, so that one day you can fly from our home and start your life. Then, too, there'll be some overlap, in between faux dependency and independence, for everyone's comfort. From which your every move will then be about *your own* adventures in the world beyond our home, maybe even with your own kids one day, no longer revolving around your mom and me. That is, if we're even included at all, except for the rare, compulsory family holiday, at which I'll tell those in your life the same old stories and share the same old photos, trying to be relevant, my heart lost in the past, reliving what will surely be the most enchanted memories of my entire life . . . of times you probably won't even remember.

Oh, doth nostalgia work fast! In my mind you were already gone, instead of three years old, inside of a Plexiglas maze. Overcome with a heart-wrenching sadness, two dripping pools of saltwater where eyes once were, with hopelessly blurred vision unable to distinguish between you and other crawling toddlers, a swelling knot in my throat . . . thinking, *WHAT HAVE I DONE?! Lost my mind?! Got a little tired so I let MY BABY scale unreachable heights in the human-hamster house? Were you really okay? Ready to be on your own? WHY THE HELL was I in such a hurry to let you drift? Was I in THAT MUCH pain? Couldn't I have been useful just a little longer? Wouldn't it have been worth it to hang around a bit more, prolonging the opportunity TO BE TOGETHER . . . before, IN THE BLINK OF AN EYE, you'd definitely not want your "Daddy" slowing you down?*

On the verge of a loud and embarrassing snort-sob, I spotted you and saw you waver. You stopped mid-tunnel. You spun around, and around again . . . and

then, hallelujah, I heard you call, "Daddy . . . ? *Daddy?!
Where are you?*" "HERE I AM!" I waved with an ex-
aggerated, ecstatic grin and eyebrows so optimisti-
cally stretched they almost left my face. *Is this really
happening?* Or was I having some delusional fantasy?
My eyes sharpening their focus, I saw yours lower to
find me, truly surprised I had left my post, *"Daddy,
WHY DID YOU LEAVE ME?"* You looked as desperate
for me as I had been feeling for you. "Daddy, *I NEED
YOU!*" My heart burst.

Faster than an Olympian track star, I entered that
human-hamster house hunched to half the height of my
almost six-foot-three-inch frame, did the loop, ripped
a few contortions to ascend the spiral climb, and leapt
over the plastic bubble pit to give you a reassuring bear
hug before you could say, "DADDY!" one more time.
Sweet redemption . . .

What *w-a-s* that?

I still don't know, but because of it, I was
reminded of how much I love you . . . and love
being loved by you. And I suddenly felt again as if all
else in my life has existed to reach this moment. Not
that any one part, including my love for your mother,
is less important, because from all those parts being
what they were, this moment was possible. This

realization suddenly illuminated all else that came before your birth in an equally glorious, meaningful light. The depth of my love for you is not merely explained and held by *your* existence, but extends to all things, all times, all places, and all the people in my life that brought us here. We are one, they are us, we are them, all is God, God is love—the very embodiment of life's greatest mystery, *answered.*

It seems so obvious now, that the world we live in is one huge human-hamster house that takes us nowhere, except within. The props and technologies we harness are far less important for what they achieve, and far more important because they give us a context in which to create, interact, and be together. It matters not whether we commute every day like the Flintstones or the Jetsons. What's important is that there are people in our lives to learn from, play with, grow with, and love.

That's what we are to each other—mirrors, sounding boards, love switches. It's the drama that makes our lives rich, that fleshes out and gives meaning to our journeys, creating reference points of relativity where none could otherwise exist. *The drama!* Oh my God, how wrong I had it.

Merit, success, money, service, dedication, innovation do not hold a candle to the treasure of emotions that make up our lives.

It's the romance of life, *created by believing in the illusions* that stirs our heart and binds our senses. Our false belief that time, space, and matter are real ultimately shows us that only our feelings last. Just as my false belief that I could lose you ratchets up my appreciation for the present moment, or my false belief that you are "my" daughter fills me with self-love and importance that I might not have otherwise allowed. These false beliefs are like temporary crutches that we will one day walk without. You've shown me this, and more.

Relishing the perfection in you, I began to consider that beyond your digits and health, what I marvel over most is your unique God-illuminated essence, which quite obviously *is present in every little girl . . . and every little boy . . . and, of course, in every grown-up.* That it *must* be there in all people, never wavering, blazing in all its glory. It could be no other way. No matter who, no matter where, no matter when, and just as important, no matter what they've ever done. They still remain of

God, by God, *pure God*. That "we are" is our saving grace, the pulsing proof of our divinity. Our magnificence does not exist because of what we do, achieve, or have. That we breathe is enough.

And then . . . when I least suspected it . . . with denial at first . . . then reluctance . . . and finally . . . a shrug . . . *I saw it in me*. I saw that *I am* the very same, pure miracle. Which is what I've written and taught others for years, yet it took my feelings for you, before I really got it about me.

This concept is still expanding in my mind. Especially getting that the love I have for you, which will never wither or fade, must be what *my* parents once felt and *still* feel for me. And more, what God once felt, and *still* must feel, for me. And that like my love for you, their love is not about what I do or don't do, who I am or who I become, not even about who or how much I serve. Their love "is" because *I am* . . . again, the very embodiment of life's greatest puzzle. Leading, therefore, to my ultimate realization:

> *I already am . . . the man you think I am.*

In fact, missing the mark is impossible. I can't not be that person, any more than you could be less than the perfection I'm constantly in awe of. *This is who we really are.* All of us. No one left behind, each a rare and precious spark of God, left to find this out for ourselves, or . . . maybe from our daughter.

Know this for yourself, precious wonder, and remember it should you ever feel unworthy of love. You're already more than you could ever hope to become. You are utterly adored simply for being who you are, exactly as you are, who you can't not be.

Without a doubt, right here and now, as you read these very words with eyes that sparkle, no matter the day, amid your dancing manifestations in a perfect world on an emerald planet while your heart beats, your blood flows, and angels peer over your shoulder, I think that you, and I, and everyone who may ever read these words, and everyone who won't, are the "luckiest" people alive.

I'll love you forever, Solecito, my little sun—

Dad

Also by Mike Dooley

Books

An Adventurer's Guide to the Jungles of Time and Space
(formerly titled *Lost in Space*)

Channeled Messages from Deep Space
(with Tracy Farquhar; formerly titled *From Deep Space with Love*)*

Choose Them Wisely: Thoughts Become Things!

The Complete Notes from the Universe

Leveraging the Universe

*Life on Earth**

Manifesting Change

*Notes from the Universe Coloring Book**

*Playing the Matrix**

*The Top 10 Things Dead People Want to Tell YOU**

Totally Unique Thoughts

Card Decks

Notes from the Universe

*Notes from the Universe on Abundance**

*Notes from the Universe on Love & Connection**

DVDs

Manifesting Change
The Path Less Traveled
Thoughts Become Things

Video Courses

The 21-Day Visualization Project (with Hope Koppelman)
Love Your Life in 30 Days (with Hope Koppelman)
*Playing the Matrix: A Laser Focused Series**
*Playing the Matrix and Getting What You Really Want**
*A Trainer's Guide to Infinite Possibilities: Certification**

For Children

Dreams Come True: All They Need Is You
Your Magical Life

*Available from Hay House

Please visit:

Hay House USA: www.hayhouse.com®
Hay House Australia: www.hayhouse.com.au
Hay House UK: www.hayhouse.co.uk
Hay House India: www.hayhouse.co.in

*For a daily dose of brief insights from Mike Dooley,
join the 900,000 people who subscribe to his free
Notes from the Universe at www.tut.com.*

Hay House Titles of Related Interest

YOU CAN HEAL YOUR LIFE, the movie,
starring Louise Hay & Friends
(available as a 1-DVD program, an expanded 2-DVD set,
and an online streaming video)
Learn more at www.hayhouse.com/louise-movie

THE SHIFT, the movie,
starring Dr. Wayne W. Dyer
(available as a 1-DVD program, an expanded 2-DVD set,
and an online streaming video)
Learn more at www.hayhouse.com/the-shift-movie

*THE TOP TEN THINGS DEAD PEOPLE WANT
TO TELL YOU,* by Mike Dooley

All of the above are available at your local bookstore,
or may be ordered by contacting Hay House (see next page).

Listen. Learn. Transform.

Listen to the audio version of this book for FREE!

Gain access to endless wisdom, inspiration, and encouragement from world-renowned authors and teachers—guiding and uplifting you as you go about your day. With the *Hay House Unlimited* Audio app, you can learn and grow in a way that fits your lifestyle . . . and your daily schedule.

With your membership, you can:

- Let go of old patterns, step into your purpose, live a more balanced life, and feel excited again.

- Explore thousands of audiobooks, meditations, immersive learning programs, podcasts, and more.

- Access exclusive audios you won't find anywhere else.

- Experience completely unlimited listening. No credits. No limits. No kidding.

Try for FREE!

Hay House Podcasts
Bring Fresh, Free Inspiration Each Week!

Hay House proudly offers a selection of life-changing
audio content via our most popular podcasts!

Hay House Meditations Podcast

Features your favorite Hay House authors guiding you through
meditations designed to help you relax and rejuvenate. Take
their words into your soul and cruise through the week!

Dr. Wayne W. Dyer Podcast

Discover the timeless wisdom of Dr. Wayne W. Dyer, world-
renowned spiritual teacher and affectionately known as "the
father of motivation." Each week brings some of the best
selections from the 10-year span of Dr. Dyer's talk show on
Hay House Radio.

Hay House Podcast

Enjoy a selection of insightful and inspiring lectures from Hay House Live
events, listen to some of the best moments from previous Hay House Radio
episodes, and tune in for exclusive interviews and behind-the-scenes audio
segments featuring leading experts in the fields of alternative health, self-
development, intuitive medicine, success, and more! Get motivated to live
your best life possible by subscribing to the free Hay House Podcast.

Find Hay House podcasts on iTunes, or visit
www.HayHouse.com/podcasts for more info.